CULT OF THE GODDESS

Social and religious change in a Hindu temple

JAMES J. PRESTON
State University of New York
College at Oneonta

Waveland Press, Inc.
Prospect Heights, Illinois

For information about this book, write or call:

Waveland Press, Inc.
P.O. Box 400
Prospect Heights, Illinois 60070
(312) 634-0081

FOREWORD

ABOUT THE AUTHOR

Dr. James J. Preston is Professor of Anthropology and Coordinator of the Religious Studies Program at the State University of New York at Oneonta. Dr. Preston has published numerous articles on various aspects of Hinduism and had edited two volumes: *Community, Self and Identity* (with Dr. B. Misra) and *Mother Worship: Theme and Variations.* His research interests span several fields in comparative religion, the study of pilgrimage, the construction of sacred icons and different aspects of religious experience. He is presently conducting field work on patterns of pilgrimage in North America.

ABOUT THE BOOK

Orissa is a major center of Hinduism. *Cult of the Goddess* is an anthropological study of religious change taking place in a Hindu Temple located in Orissa's largest city. Here a once small neighbourhood goddess temple has suddenly grown to become the most widely attended religious institution in the city. The book explores the inner workings of this temple and illustrates the importance of goddess worship.

Cult of the Goddess is an unusual ethnographic description of Orissan Hinduism as experienced by an American anthropologist. The book is an additional testimony to the great flexibility of Hinduism. Even under conditions of intense internal conflicts, this small shrine devoted to goddess Chandi emerges triumphant. Unlike other temples that have been torn apart by internal strife, this shrine has managed to become a thriving center of popular Hinduism. Devotion to the goddess assists newly urbanized people as they adjust to new conditions imposed by city life.

PREFACE TO THE INDIAN EDITION

The study presented here is based on anthropological fieldwork conducted from 1972 to 1973 in Cuttack City, Orissa, India. It is part of the author's larger, continuing research interest in changing aspects of Hinduism. This preliminary report represents only a portion of the data collected in Orissa. Though the original research included information on both urban and rural temples, the present study focuses exclusively on Chandi Temple in the city of Cuttack. By selecting a single institution in a large urban center it has been possible to observe the interplay of several key variables influencing religious change in India. The impact of urbanism, new secular patrons, and emerging popular styles of Hinduism on a religious institution can be profound. Many temples have declined under pressures of change. Chandi Temple is flourishing.

Another focus of interest here is the *Shakta* cult of contemporary Orissa. It would be presumptuous to attempt a full study of this complex phenomenon in this short volume. Nor is there sufficient historical or ethnographic data to develop a comprehensive picture of Orissan goddess worship. The study presented here brings together some basic information on the topic, with particular focus on how the goddess cult becomes manifested at Chandi Temple. Goddess worship seems particularly suited to the needs of newly urbanized individuals.

Thus, Chandi Temple is located at the confluence of several socio-religious streams in contemporary Hinduism. It does not represent the full range of factors emerging today as prime movers that impact on religion in modern India. Other temples in different parts of the subcontinent would certainly reflect a large variety of other social, cultural, economic, and religious variables at work. Nevertheless, it is felt that this study has certain unusual characteristics to offer the student of religious change. Chandi Temple is *not* a large pilgrimage center or ancient sacred complex. Yet, there are thousands of middle range, relatively recent shrines like Chandi Temple in India's cities. None of them has been studied ethnographically in any detail.

Also, significant here is the relationship of the Hindu Religious Endowment Commission to the resolution of conflicts within temples. Little is known about these new bureaucratic patrons. Particularly important is the problem of how religious institutions will survive as they become less dependent on economic support from landed properties. The old feudal pattern has changed and many temples are being profoundly affected by such changes.

Research on change often suffers from lack of periodic restudies. The present study is no exception. It is recognized that Chandi Temple has undergone many changes since 1973. The author is grateful to the American Council of Learned Societies, the National Endowment for the Humanities, and the State University of New York for financial assistance to return to India in 1979. Though this brief journey was intended primarily for attending an international meeting, it was possible to spend several weeks in Orissa. At that time additional information was collected at Chandi Temple. Thus, some of the impressions formulated by the author since 1973 have been tested six years later.

Fieldwork often requires special sensitivities on the part of the researcher. These sensitivities, however, bear no fruit without the good will and kindness of many people. The author is grateful for the special assistance received by friends, government officials, and university colleagues in Orissa. They were always cordial and enthusiastic about the focus of the study. The staff at Chandi Temple spent long hours answering questions and revealing some of their deepest thoughts about the institution. The Board of Trustees, Executive Officer, and temple priests opened themselves to the scrutiny of social science research. Particular credit is due to Sri Lokanath Panda who spent much precious time explaining and demonstrating the Tantric rites associated with *Shakta* tradition. This study would have been impossible without his many hours of assistance.

JAMES J. PRESTON

PREFACE TO THE WAVELAND 1985 EDITION

The study of Chandi Temple was one of the first attempts by a non-Indian anthropologist to shed light on the complex ritual and social life in the temples of contemporary Hinduism. Since the Indian edition of *Cult of the Goddess* was first published (1980) there have been several new studies of Hindu temples conducted by anthropologists. Unfortunately, some South Asian specialists act as though their part of India is isolated from the rest of the subcontinent. Consequently, scholars who study temples in one part of the subcontinent do not cite publications of research in other regions of South Asia. This lack of an all-India research effort to piece together the complex web of religious institutions leaves a great gap in our theoretical understanding of Indian temples.

In the last several years a rich literature on Hindu temples has begun to emerge. Indian anthropologists have contributed excellent research on temples along the Ganges River, particularly in the holy city of Benares. Some of the largest temples are located in south India. These are becoming significant loci of research among specialists for this region. In Orissa, and eastern India in general, there is a growing body of literature on all phases of temple life; most noteworthy being the extensive German Research Project that has focused on the Orissan Jagannath cult and its elaborate temple complex. There are studies of temples in Nepal which suggest an even broader South Asian approach to the topic. All these studies represent an international scholarly effort with research contributions from England, India, Germany, and America. This flurry of research activity needs to be integrated, in order to develop a comprehensive perspective on the whole network of religious institutions in the subcontinent; an ambitious task that remains to be undertaken by South Asian specialists at some time in the future. It is hoped the popular publication of this modest study of a middle range Hindu temple will help contribute to a broader appreciation of the challenge that Hinduism in general, and temple studies in particular, presents to the anthropological study of religion.

This book was written originally for undergraduates and other interested readers who are not specialists in South Asian studies. For this reason most Sanskrit and Oriya words have been omitted from the text. Unfortunately, a majority of writings on Hinduism are so heavily burdened with complex foreign terminology that students interested in this fascinating phenomenon become lost and frustrated. Therefore, I have intentionally tried to describe the complex ceremonies and rituals encountered in India with language easily comprehendable to the general educated reader.

Much has been written about Hinduism for general consumption from a philosophical point of view. Yet few books are available on the actual practice of this great religion as it is lived in the everyday world. In this small volume I have attempted to bring alive, in a terse format, the practice of Hinduism in the fabric of Indian life. Here we see the complex dialectic between ancient traditions and forces of modernism unfolding within an urban Hindu temple. This volume provides an opportunity for American students to have a glimpse into the inner workings of one of the great world religions, to explore the meaning of religion in the lives of the people of India and to discover how goddess worship continues to thrive in the modern world. It reveals also the value of the anthropological approach for the comparative study of religion.

The American edition of *Cult of the Goddess* has been made possible by Vikas Publishing House who released the rights to the author. I am grateful this volume has been published both in India and the United States so it can reach the widest possible international readership.

James J. Preston
Oneonta, New York

ACKNOWLEDGEMENTS

I wish to express my appreciation to Dr. Bhabagrahi Misra whose guidance and support made this study possible. Also, special thanks are due to Professor Cora Du Bois for many helpful suggestions in the analysis and presentation of the data from Chandi Temple. I owe a debt of gratitude to the following individuals who offered encouragement in the preparation of this manuscript: Dr. James Freeman, Dr. Milton Singer, Dr. Ena Campbell, Dr. Leighton McCutchen and Dr. Frank Blackford. The present study was made possible with financial aid from the Hartford Seminary Foundation and a Research Assistantship from Harvard University. I am especially grateful to Professor L.K. Mahapatra, Chairman of the Department of Anthropology, Uktal University for providing research affiliation status during fieldwork in Orissa. The following friends and acquaintances in Orissa deserve special mention for their many hours of advice and support: Dr. K.C. Panigrahi, Sri Nilamani Senapati (ICS), Sri Sudhansu Mohapatra, Sri S.P. Mahanti, Sri P.C. Nayak, and Ms. Debbie Swallow. I am also deeply indebted to my wife, Carolyn, for her immeasurable assistance both in the field and the preparation of the final manuscript for publication. The many details that go into typing were skillfully and patiently managed by Mrs. Robin Whitbeck and Mrs. Hilda Mercun. Finally, I would like to thank Mr. Ron Embling and his staff for assistance with some of the graphics included in the volume.

It is the people of Orissa, however, who deserve most credit for this book. They invited me into their sacred temples, treated me with respect and gave many hours of their time to make this study possible. On several occasions temple priests told me that I had been sent to India by the goddess as an envoy to carry her divine message to America and the world. Though this is a formidable charge, I accept it with humility and dedicate this book to the people of Orissa, in hope, above all, that it is worthy of their trust and respect.

For Dr. Bhabagrahi Misra—professor, colleague, and friend

CONTENTS

A folk painting of Orissa's major deity, Jagannath, Lord of the World.

One form of the goddess is Laksmi who represents good fortune and wealth. Here she is portrayed in an idyllic setting, emerging out of a lotus blossom.

Devotees can purchase thousands of images of deities in local shops to place in their homes. Here the goddess Kali is portrayed with a garland of demon skulls about her neck. The priest is offering flowers and meat to satisfy her hunger for blood.

A benign form of the goddess as Saraswati, associated with music, learning, and culture. Each year she is worshipped during a special ceremony especially by students and teachers who wish to enhance their skills.

One of over a hundred life-size statues made each year during Durga Puja. Here Lord Shiva is portrayed with his consort, goddess Parvati and Nandi, the sacred bull.

Another life-size display of clay statues found along the streets in neighborhood shelters during Durga Puja. Lord Shiva presides with his wife Parvati at his feet.

A scene with Lord Shiva protecting his wife, the goddess Parvati, from a moustached demon. In the foreground a Brahmin prepares an evening puja during Durga Puja.

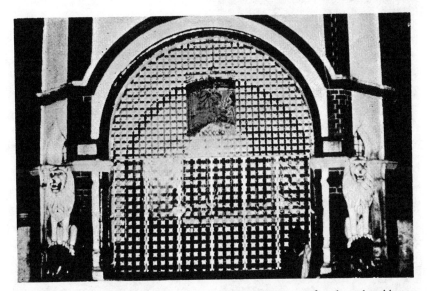

On the last day of Durga Puja over one hundred mud images of gods and goddesses are carried from different neighborhoods of Cuttack to this road-side shrine near the home of the Rani of Darpani. Here they are judged. The best one wins a prize. Then the images are carried to the Mahanadi river where they are submerged by devotees in an atmosphere of joy and abandonment.

Shiva and Parvati reign supreme. These life-size mud statues are commissioned by groups of students, merchants, neighborhood groups, and wealthy people of Cuttack City.

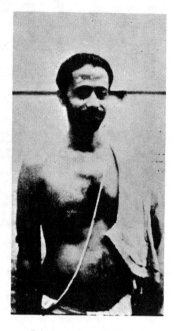

Priests are preparing to
worship the goddess during
Durga Puja.

Priest at Chandi Temple.

Main entrance to the temple. The neon lights are a recent addition.

A typical photograph of Satya Sai Baba found in the homes of thousands of devotees in Cuttack City. This living saint claims to be an avatar of Vishnu, Shiva, and the Great Goddess, all in one. He is known for working miracles and is particularly popular among merchants and young people.

During Durga Puja the goddess is dressed in a new form each evening. Here she appears as the ten-armed Mahisamardini Durga, Conqueror of the Buffalo Demon, Mahisasura.

A wandering Brahmin who blesses people wherever he meets them by placing a mark of red vermillion paste on their foreheads in exchange for a small donation.

Temples are like second homes to wandering ascetics. This old man travels from one shrine to another, accepting support from more permanent members of the temple community.

ONE

INTRODUCTION

HINDUISM IS ONE OF THE WORLD'S MOST COMPLEX RELIGIONS. It is composed of tightly-knit myths, rites and customs which have evolved from prehistoric times. An interesting feature of this ancient religion is the worship of mother goddesses. These female deities continue to play an important role in the popular religion of modern India. While Hinduism manifests certain common characteristics throughout the subcontinent, there are important regional variations. Goddess worship, for example, is found everywhere in India, but is most highly concentrated in the eastern states of Orissa, Bengal and Assam, where yearly festivals to Durga, the Great Goddess, flourish with unparalleled pomp and ceremony.

The present study was conducted in an urban goddess temple in the state of Orissa. This region has remained somewhat isolated from the mainstream of modern Indian life, but for centuries devout Hindus have visited Orissan shrines while traveling along a major pilgrimage route which extends from Bengal, through Orissa, and south toward Tamilnadu.

The Orissan Context

Despite the fact that Orissa's economy remains relatively underdeveloped, it continues to be an important center of religious history. The great emperor Ashoka decided to fight his last war in Orissa.[1] Every major religious sect of Hinduism has taken root in Orissan soil and flourished at some point in time. The treacherous coastal river valleys and remote tribal mountains have acted as natural barriers to foreign invaders. Both Muslim and British rule of India came late to Orissa, leaving the indigenous infrastructure relatively unchanged.

Today Orissa covers about 60,000 square miles along the Bay of Bengal in eastern India. The state is naturally divided into two main parts, the western mountains largely populated

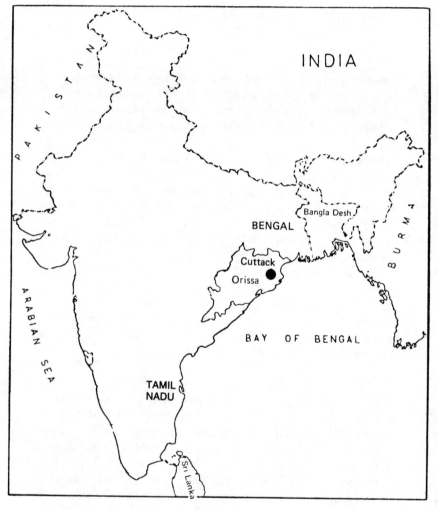

INDIA

PAKISTAN

BENGAL

Bangla Desh

Cuttack

Orissa

BURMA

ARABIAN SEA

BAY OF BENGAL

TAMIL
NADU

Sri Lanka

MAP 1

by tribal peoples and the coastal lowlands of the east where Hinduism has been entrenched for thousands of years. Most of the population lives in this eastern delta region; a rich rice-growing country with many villages connected by a series of intricate canals and roadways. Almost every year Orissa suffers devastating cyclonic storms, droughts, floods, famines or epidemics. Despite these natural calamities large numbers of pilgrims from all over India annually flock to Orissa's famous temple of Jagannath at Puri.

Though Orissa is one of India's poorest states, some progress has been made in the fields of health, education, and welfare. Twenty years ago these public services were almost nonexistent. Today, a spreading cash economy, modern medicine, and expanding transportation services have opened new opportunities for different segments of the population. Still, there is little industry in Orissa, few urban centers, and large untapped natural resources.

Religious Change

Religion is more than a mere system of rites and symbols. There is no way to isolate the sacred world of temples and priests from the community. This is particularly true in India, where it is difficult to draw clear lines to distinguish sacred from secular domains. Religion is part of culture, integrating man, nature, and cosmos, with the common problems of everyday life. Anthropologists have been long interested in how religion operates in the process of culture change.

There is a debate among South Asian specialists about the role of religion in the modernization of India. Some anthropologists suggest that Hinduism is essentially conservative and slow to change. Others report evidence that religious institutions are declining with the onslaught of urbanization and modernism.[2] Several recent studies, however, have shed new light on the phenomenon. It is argued in these studies that modern and traditional cultures are not necessarily incompatible. Singer's (1972 : 384) comprehensive study of the social and religious institutions of Madras city suggests that traditionalism may act as a major vehicle for modernization. A similar conclusion is reached by Freeman's (1975) work on religion in village

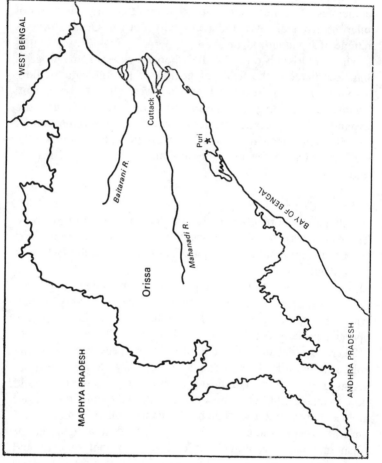

MAP 2: *The State of Orissa*

Orissa. Miller and Wertz (1976: xiii) expressed this same point in their work on the monasteries of Bhubaneswar. "In India what appears to be a new emphasis may actually be a revival of an ancient practice or belief. Instead of moving toward secularization, people may be simply shifting their values and reorganizing their institutions."

The present study extends this new view of the role of religion in the modernizing process by illustrating how an urban goddess temple can act as a spearhead for change. From this point of view Hindu religious institutions are neither doomed to extinction, nor necessarily resistant to change.[3] They vary greatly in their adaptive capacities. While some temples are clearly outmoded, others have managed to create a new synthesis to cope with change.

One reason it has been so difficult to comprehend how Hinduism fits into the larger pattern of change in India is the relatively few research projects which have been conducted on temples. This dearth of research on the institutional base of Hinduism is partly due to barriers of entry into sacred shrines for non-Hindus. Also significant here is the fact that many Indian anthropologists who would have access to temples have been preoccupied with studies of tribal people. In recent years, however, both Indian and foreign anthropologists are turning their attention to religious institutions.[4]

A Place to Begin

The present study is concerned with changing patterns of patronage, symbolism, and life-styles associated with a growing urban goddess temple in coastal Orissa. Several questions are raised: What role does this religious institution play in the city of Cuttack? Is there something unique about goddess worship to attract the increasing number of devotees who attend this temple each year? How does goddess worship in Orissa fit into the larger mosaic of India as a whole? Is Singer (1972 : 404) correct when he asserts that traditionalism in India is *not* opposed to innovation, change or modernity? Chandi Temple was selected to answer these questions because of its strategic position in the religious life of Cuttack, Orissa's largest city.[5] The Goddess Chandi is recognized by the people of Cuttack as their presiding deity. In recent years she has come to play

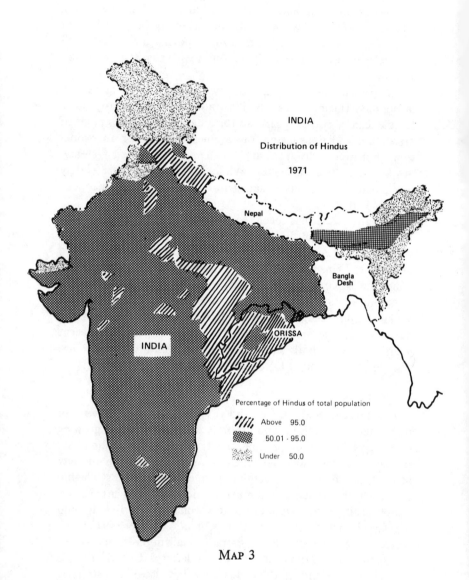

INDIA

Distribution of Hindus

1971

Nepal

Bangla
Desh

ORISSA

INDIA

Percentage of Hindus of total population

Above   95.0

50.01 - 95.0

Under   50.0

MAP 3

an important role in the ritual, economic, and social life of the city.

It is recognized that there are serious limitations to the study of a single religious institution. For this reason a survey of both urban and rural goddess temples was conducted in the coastal part of Orissa. Also, in addition to Chandi Temple, several other religious institutions in Cuttack were investigated. This was done to provide a larger comparative framework for the study of Chandi Temple, which can only be understood when contrasted with other religious institutions, both within Cuttack, and in the surrounding region.

It is assumed that many of the social forces at work in the city of Cuttack are also operating in the temple. Nevertheless, it would be erroneous to engage in extensive generalizations about Cuttack city based on the study of a single temple. In the first place the temple has religious and social configurations that are peculiar to it. Nor are certain castes found represented in the spectrum of participants in the life of the temple. The investigation of a single key institution is not offered here as a solution to the problem of studying the complexity of urban life. The study of cities, religious sects, and of social change, requires sophisticated multilevel strategies. Chandi Temple is only a convenient place to begin.

It is unfortunate, yet necessary, for the social scientist to artificially divide a complex whole, such as a religious system, into its component parts. Analysis inevitably results in a degree of distortion. However, a well-balanced presentation of the parts of the system should serve to minimize much of this distortion. For this reason the pattern of religious change in Chandi Temple presented here has been deliberately segmented into three main components, each part carefully balanced to illustrate the ultimate integrity of the system as a whole. Equal emphasis is placed on the temple's social structure, the symbolic system, and the congregation of worshippers. Thus, the threads of religious change are traced at several levels within the institution. Since Chandi Temple is a focal point in the religious life of Cuttack, it is instructive to extend the analysis beyond the inner workings of the institution to reveal how goddess worship fits into the ritual network of Cuttack city.

The following chapters begin with a discussion of goddess worship as a religious theme in India. The framework acts as a background for the specific variant on this theme found in Orissa, and more specifically at Chandi Temple. Next is an extensive discussion of the evolution of patronage at Chandi Temple. Then we enter the inner sanctuary of the temple to observe the ritual process, focusing particularly on the ceremony of animal sacrifice. This leads to a chapter on the religious experiences of devotees. Here special attention is given to the intervention of the goddess in the lives of worshippers. How do people relate to her? What needs does she fill in their lives? Why do they worship a female deity? Next is a discussion of how Chandi Temple fits into the broader context of Cuttack city in particular, and Hinduism in general; what does this temple tell us about the role of mother worship in the process of religious change? Finally, the concluding chapter returns to theoretical issues about the study of religious change in the Indian subcontinent.

TWO

MOTHER WORSHIP

EVIDENCE OF GODDESS WORSHIP EXTENDS BACK AT LEAST 30,000 years to Neolithic times. All across Europe small figurines of female deities have been unearthed by archaeologists. These highly stylized statues place special emphasis on the breasts and genitals of the goddess, suggesting an early association with fertility rites. Mother worship appears to have been nearly universal. It formed an important component of the religions of pre-Christian Europe. Goddess cults thrived in ancient Greece and Rome. They also flourished in Ireland, Germanic Europe and among the ancient Hebrews.

The worship of female images continues to survive throughout the world. In modern Europe many shrines to the Virgin Mary are built where earlier goddess cults once existed. Pilgrimage centers associated with the madonna are notorious for their miraculous efficacy. Devotees from all over the world flock to these sacred shrines devoted to mother worship. Next to Rome the largest place of Christian pilgrimage in the world is the grotto at Lourdes. Here the healing waters are said to cure hundreds of invalids of various ailments each year.

The Virgin has also played an important role in the New World where she has been a focus of ethnic identity for millions of people. In Mexico, for example, the Virgin of Guadalupe represents a unique combination of indigenous Indian and Spanish cultures. Here the ancient Indian goddess Tonantzin and the Spanish madonna have been fused into a powerful symbol of Mexican nationalism. As protectress of the oppressed and downtrodden, the Virgin of Guadalupe became a symbol of unification and a focus for the Mexican Independence movement (Campbell 1982).

Though mother worship takes many different forms the world over, certain common features are evident at the level of human need. People usually turn to female deities to be healed, to assure abundant harvests, or for relief from many kinds of physical and spiritual suffering. All these qualities are also found in the various manifestations of the Indian mother goddesses. However, unlike the Christian madonnas, Hindu goddesses may be worshipped exclusively in their own right. They are usually *not* intercessors between human beings and a masculine deity. Even in the few cases where they function this way, informants are clear about the independent power and legitimacy of goddesses as manifestations of the divinity.

Indian Mother Goddesses

Mother worship has ancient roots in South Asian prehistory. Terracotta figurines of goddesses dated as early as 3,000 B.C. have been found in the Indus Valley Civilization. There is evidence that female deities were worshipped at different levels of intensity throughout the evolution of Hinduism. It appears, however, that devotion to the goddess emerged as a distinct cult of considerable strength some time during the seventh century A.D. (Chattopadyaya 1970 : 144).

The gods most frequently worshipped in Hinduism are Siva and several manifestations of Vishnu. Numerous sects have developed around these male deities, stressing different styles of devotion. Equal importance is given to the Great Goddess who takes many forms, both benign and malevolent. As Saraswati she is the symbol of learning and culture. In her manifestation as Laksmi she represents good fortune, wealth and luxury. When she is Kali or Durga people both fear and respect her. In this aspect she is capable of great vengeance against those who would cross her. Kali demands blood sacrifices to symbolize her strength as the archenemy of the demons. As Sitala the goddess is able to either cause or cure diseases, particularly smallpox and cholera. Then there are the many small *gramdevis* (village goddesses) found in most Indian villages. Here the goddess is mother of her people, protecting India's vulnerable villages from enemies and natural disasters.

While most goddess shrines are small and inconspicuous, many others have developed into famous pilgrimage centers attracting thousands of devotees each year. These larger temples are mapped out in the sacred literature and integrated into the Hindu Great Tradition through the Legend of Sati. This myth explains the distribution of these temples in India by tying them together as different parts of the spiritual body of the supreme Mother Goddess. According to this legend, Sati, the wife of Lord Siva, was unhappy because she had not been invited to a sacrificial ceremony held by her father, Daksa Prajapati. Sati decided to attend without an invitation. This resulted in an embarrassing scene where she was publically insulted. As a result of this social injury she died of despair. When the news of her death reached Lord Siva, he became furious and hastened to the scene. There he decapitated Daksa Prajapati. After this Siva was completely mad and wandered about the earth in profound grief, dancing furiously with the dead body of his beloved wife on his shoulders. The gods were alarmed that Siva was distracted from his usual meditation, so they conspired to free him of his madness by spiritually entering into Sati's body through yoga and dividing it into many pieces which fell from the shoulders of Siva on different parts of India (*Matsya Purana*).

The places where Sati's body fell to the earth are known as *sakti pithas*. These are sacred pilgrimage sites associated with the goddess. Many of the *pithas* mentioned in the Puranas do not exist today. The number of *pithas* varies from 52 to 108 in different sacred texts. These sacred places are scattered throughout South Asia, forming the focal points in the sacred geography of Indian mother worship. The temple of goddess Kamakhya in the state of Assam is particularly sacred because this is where Sati's *yoni* (vagina) is believed to have fallen to the earth. In this way the major goddess temples of India are linked to the Great Tradition of Hinduism through identification with a *sakti pitha*. The Legend of Sati might have originally served as a device to integrate diverse tribal and Buddhist goddesses under the umbrella of the Hindu pantheon (Sircar 1948 : 3). Thus, diverse elements of the Little Tradition are woven into the mainstream of Hinduism through identification with *sakti pithas* and the Great Goddess.

Another legend explains the origin of the goddess Durga. In this myth (*Markandeya Purana*) the goddess was created by the combined energies of all the gods. Emanating from her divine creators, the goddess emerges as a powerful force released on a world which is threatened by domination from demons. Only through the cooperation of the male deities is it possible to vanquish the powerful forces of evil in the world. Here the goddess as Durga is a consummate warrior. She is part mother because she protects her devotees and part malevolent witch in her capacity as enemy of evil, capable of immense cruelty and destruction. Here is the root cause of the great ambivalence which is felt by devotees about this form of the mother goddess.

According to Babb (1975: 226) the benign and malevolent features in the Indian goddess are reflections of an interesting opposition in the relationship between male and female categories in the divinity; "When female dominates male the pair is sinister; when male dominates female the pair is benign." For this reason goddesses like Parvati and Sita, who are dominated by their male counterparts, emphasize the passive features of the feminine. While Kali, who is sometimes depicted standing with her foot on the corpse of her consort Lord Siva, is a representation of the aggressive potential of the female when she becomes dominant. Obviously under different conditions these two aspects of the goddess, represented in various manifestations, have equally positive contributions to make. Not only are the goddesses capable of love and nurturance, they are also a source of justice, playing an important role in the constant struggle between good and evil which permeates the condition of man. Thus, devotees may look to a goddess for the promise of new birth and for the restitution of injustice due to oppression and the cruelty of fate.

Goddesses are often portrayed as earth mothers identified with the fertility of fields. This is particularly true for the goddess Durga. In this form the goddess and the earth are identical. As symbol of fertility the goddess is treated as though she were a pregnant woman. In some of the earliest iconography, for example, she is portrayed as a woman giving birth. In Assam the goddess Kamakhya has monthly menstrual rites. On these occasions Kamakhya temple is closed to the public so the deity may rest. Frequently Durga, and the more malevolent goddess Kali, are recipients of blood sacrifices; associating blood, earth and fertility.

The goddess is also manifested as a disease deity when she appears as Sitala, Goddess of Smallpox, or Mangala, Goddess of Fever. It is believed that these deities can both cause the illness and cure it. Complex rituals are performed to cool Sitala's wrath. Some devotees become possessed by her. Possession and trance are part of an elaborate ritual complex designed to control the spread of smallpox, which has taken so many thousands of lives in the subcontinent. The goddess Sitala acts as both a potential instrument of death and a source of hope for frightened devotees.

Goddesses also play many other roles in Indian life. They are asked to intercede in virtually every imaginable set of circumstances. Barren women fast and worship various goddesses in order to become pregnant. People ask for solutions to financial problems and for protection in relationships with adversaries. Thus, goddesses are at once mothers, protectresses, and mediators. One surrenders with ease to a goddess who offers some degree of hope in the face of overwhelming tragedy. A history of constant suffering from oppression, combined with endemic natural disasters which constantly threaten the delicate balance of the agricultural cycle, produces an atmosphere of submission and surrender in the subcontinent. No wonder the Indian mother goddess is a beacon of hope and a source of renewal for her people.

There is a connection between the role of women in Indian life and the special position of female deities in the Hindu pantheon. Though Indian women are supposed to be absolutely devoted to their husbands, who are respected as embodiments of the deity, women may also reign supreme in their own domain as mothers of their children. Motherhood is regarded with great respect in India. At one time certain women were worshipped as manifestations of the divine. Eliade (1958: 203) reveals the symbolic value of the feminine in the following passage,

Thus woman comes to symbolize the irreducibility of the sacred and the divine, the inapprehensible essence of the ultimate reality. Woman incarnates both the mystery of creation and the mystery of Being, of everything that *is*, that incomprehensibly becomes and dies and is reborn.

The sacred quality of the feminine is evident in Indian village life, where women spend a considerable amount of time fasting, worshipping local deities, and preparing for numerous minor festivals. In most parts of India the ritual cycle includes several monthly ceremonies meant for women alone. This is one way that women socialize and make contact with relatives in nearby villages.

In eastern India whole villages may worship goddesses almost exclusively. A devotee of the goddess is known as a *Shakta* (goddess worshipper). Members of this cult cut across caste lines, though frequently devotees are from lower castes. *Shaktas* perform precise rites with strong magical overtones. The unique feature of this brand of Hinduism is its "life affirming" quality. The *Shakta* cult emphasizes total involvement with life. Nothing is excluded. Even the sexual impulse must be accepted, transformed, and harmonized for one to attain spiritual realization. The fundamental idea here is that the human body is a microcosm and the universe is the macrocosm. Since the physical body is believed to be the abode of Ultimate Truth, it is the perfect instrument for the integration of the male and female principles. "The one which becomes two constantly aspires to become one again" (Mookerjee 1971:16). Everything has an outer and inner reality for the devotee of the goddess. From the outer view the sexual act may appear to be perverse, but from the inner view the same act signifies creation—a moment of divinity. The two views are only different aspects of the same reality.

This "life affirming" quality of the *Shakta* cult is evident in its special liturgy, the *pancamakara puja*. Until the early part of the twentieth century there were two subsects of *Shaktas*. One sect interpreted the sacraments literally, sometimes worshipping a nude female as the goddess. The other took the rites metaphorically. The five sacraments in the *pancamakara puja* include (1) *mansa* (the eating of meat), (2) *maithuna* (sexual union), (3) *matsya* (the eating of fish), (4) *madya* (drinking of wine), and (5) *Mudra* (ritual hand gestures). The more liberal sect of *Shaktas* sat in a circle with their female counterparts and actually engaged in these practices, while the conservative sect would only use symbolic substitutes. Eyewitness accounts of the sect that actually engaged in sexual union are rare because these rites were cloaked with considerable secrecy. Nineteenth-century observers have reported the orgiastic quality of this liturgy, but the extent of its practice is unknown. A rich iconography, however, depicts males and females engaging in sexual union on many of India's temples. According to sacred texts, this mystical eroticism should be practiced ceremonially, accompanied by elaborate acts of purification and prayers. It is a symbolic enactment of the union of opposites. The woman is changed into an incarnation of the goddess, as *Shakti,* and the man becomes the male deity, *Siva.* Thus, sexual union is spiritually transformed as the human couple become divine. This is not an egoistic satisfaction of sexual urges, but rather an act of transcendence, where ideally the male's sperm does not ejaculate. The emphasis is on *control* through yoga, not on pleasure or release. Through control of the senses the couple attains a higher spiritual ecstasy. Few traces of these rites are found today. Wine and ritualized sexual union are absent from the ceremony, though meat and fish may be eaten. This change in the sacraments associated with contemporary goddess worship does not imply that it is less life oriented than before. Only the external ritual expression seems to have changed, dropping the sexual and sensuous overtones to satisfy puritanical elements in Indian society which arose in the early twentieth century.

A survey of temples conducting various Tantric rites today would inevitably reveal a broad range of substitutions employed in contemporary performances of the *pancamakara puja.* At Jagannath temple in Puri, for instance, each component part of the original five sacraments has a specific symbolic substitute: *matsya* (fish) is represented by specially prepared green vegetables, *mansa* (meat) is symbolized by ginger, *madya* (wine) is substituted with green coconut water, *maithuna* (sexual union) consists of dancing by *devadasis* (temple dancers), and *mudras* (ritual hand gestures) are represented by a preparation of sugar and flour (Mishra 1971: 153). At the same shrine worship of the goddess Bimala (consort of Jagannath) involves less extreme substitutions. Fish are offered, and a ram is sacrificed to this goddess at certain times of year. In many temples the original five sacraments have been largely displaced through different phases of sublimation and transposition of symbols.

Orissan Goddesses

Hinduism is not uniform in the subcontinent. There are significant regional and local variations which must be taken into account. Goddess worship is no exception to this general rule.

Orissan goddesses share all the characteristics of female deities found throughout India. Nevertheless, certain unique Orissan characteristics are evident; goddess shrines are frequently, though not always, linked into the Jagannath cult at Puri. Orissan goddesses often retain strong characteristics of tribal deities. Village level goddesses reflect local religious traditions, particular to Orissa. Regional goddesses frequently represent the combination of tribal and Sanskritic elements fused together by Orissa's feudal rajas who used these goddesses, along with both Brahmin and non-Brahmin priests, to forge centers of political power. These tutelary goddesses of Orissa's princes continue to perpetuate strong regional customs identified with specific kingdoms.

The people of India worship more than one deity. Goddess worship is almost always part of a larger, more intricate pattern of religious symbolism. Hinduism in Orissa is strongly eclectic and clear lines delineating one sect from another are absent. A devotee of the goddess almost always spends a portion of his day worshipping Siva, Jagannath, or other male deities. This blending of deities and religious traditions results in a complex interlocking symbolic network.

An accurate history of goddess worship is impossible to reconstruct from the fragmentary evidence available. Still, sacred texts suggest the prevalence of the goddess cult in the early history of Orissa. The writings of Sarala Das, celebrated author of Oriya literature, illustrates this point. This great poet wrote a special version of the *Mahabharata* in the fifteenth century A.D. Sarala's rendition of this famous epic was important because it was the first major Sanskrit text to be interpreted into Oriya, the principal language of Orissa. The author's strong devotion to the goddess is reflected in his unique conviction that she is the supreme source of power, even greater than her consort Lord Siva. This unorthodox interpretation of the relationship between male and female aspects of the divinity could never have found acceptance unless an already well-established tradition of goddess worship existed.

Throughout Orissa today goddesses continue to play an important role in the religious life of the people. For three days each year in the month of June there is a unique cluster of rites performed in most of the villages near the coast. At this time

Laksmi, the Goddess of Wealth, is believed to be "ready for breeding." But first this goddess, who represents the earth, is put on a strict vegetarian diet of fruit and wheat cakes. This symbolizes the beginning of her menstrual cycle. The goddess, like the village women, does not bathe or eat rice for three days while she remains in a state of ritual pollution. On the fourth day she is given a bath and becomes "ready for breeding." Unmarried girls do not walk barefoot on the earth during this time in order to honor the menstruation of the goddess. Also, men refrain from tilling the soil. All village work comes to a halt. On the fourth day when the menstrual period is complete, there is great festivity in the villages. Special songs are reserved for this occasion. It is a time to visit relatives, attend dancing parties or local dramatic performances that last into the night. Here we see the strong identification of village women with the goddess and the earth.

The goddess temples of coastal Orissa represent a broad range of structural and symbolic variations. And though there are basic similarities, they differ widely with respect to caste composition, patterns of patronage and the social backgrounds of devotees. In order to assess these variables it is necessary to conduct a symbolic network analysis using survey methods.[1] One way to survey a regional sect is to visit a selection of its major and minor temples. I did this in 1972 to construct a larger picture of the Orissan variant of goddess worship. This was a necessary preliminary to the study of Chandi Temple in Cuttack. The fourteen temples surveyed represented only a fraction of the goddess shrines in coastal Orissa. However, the temples selected were considered by the people to be the most important centers of goddess worship in the region. This suggests that the sample is representative of at least the major pilgrimage temples devoted to female deities.

The survey revealed three types of goddess temple. These were directly correlated with different geographic regions in the state. It was found that temples located near the eastern coast were characterized by dominant Brahmin castes, vegetarian deities, absence of animal sacrifice and strong ties to the Jagannath cult at Puri. A distinct contrast was observed in temples located near the inland mountains. These were distinguished by dominant non-Brahmin priests, non-vegetarian deities, animal

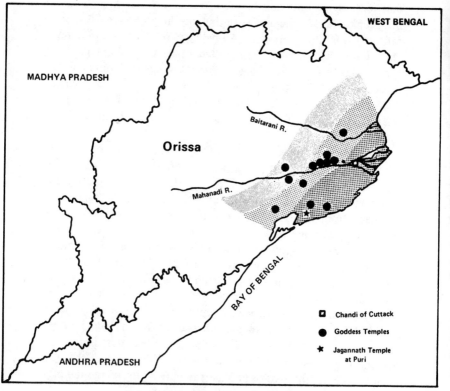

MAP 4: *Goddess Temples in Orissa*

sacrifice and independence of links with the Jagannath complex
on the coast.

A third type of temple was found in a middle zone between
these two extremes. These temples displayed a mixture of
Brahmin and non-Brahmin features. For example, in some cases
the goddess was both vegetarian and non-vegetarian at different
times of year. In these temples the opposition between castes
was reconciled by developing a variety of different compromises
at the symbolic level.

The results of this survey are easy to explain. The inland part
of Orissa has strong tribal roots. Many of the people here were
absorbed into Hinduism within the last several hundred years.
This is probably the main reason for the prevalence of the non-
Brahmin style of worshipping the goddess, with its associated
animal sacrifice and independence from Jagannath at Puri. By
contrast, temples on the coast are located along the piligrimage
corridor where there is a long history of Hinduism, with a pre-
ponderance of Brahmins and well-established ties to Hinduism
in other parts of India.

Despite this apparent cleavage there is still a considerable
amount of variation in styles of goddess worship throughout
Orissa. Each temple has evolved its own unique combination of
local and regional symbols. Yet, it is not enough to emphasize
the heterogeneity of goddess worship in Orissa. Common themes
are not difficult to find. Goddesses everywhere are propitiated for
relief from disease, famine, death or other natural disasters
which are endemic in the state. Also, everywhere devotees report
an attitude of surrender to the deity. This is the prime goal of
goddess worship—surrender to the deity in exchange for her
benevolent protection and good fortune.

Though the goddess temples of Orissa are important to the
local people, only a few of them have attained all-India fame.
In Orissa only the temples of the goddess Bimala at Puri, Biraja
at Jajpur, and Bhubaneswari at Bhubaneswar are mentioned as
pithas in the classical Sanskrit literature. Priests at other temples
in Orissa, however, assert that their temples are legitimate places
where parts of the Great Goddess fell to earth. The best known
of these is the temple of Biraja located on the Baitarani River.
This temple's notoriety is due to its status as one of the *pithas*
(pilgrimage shrines) of the sacred Hindu texts. It is believed

by the local people that this temple is located where the navel of Sati fell to earth after parts of her body were scattered throughout India. The navel of the Great Goddess is symbolized by a deep well which is located inside a small shrine within the temple compound. A local tradition asserts that this well is connected to the Ganges River at Benares by underground rivers located deep beneath the earth. Benares is several hundred miles to the north of this temple (Preston 1983a: 243). The convention of establishing authority for a local tradition through mythological connections with the waters of the Ganges has been noted elsewhere in Orissa and other parts of India (Miller and Wertz 1976 : 9 and Clothey 1972 : 91).

The Rise of Durga

The cities of Orissa have recently witnessed a rapid increase in the Bengali style of worshipping the goddess as Durga in the month of October (Freeman 1975: 129; Miller and Wertz 1976: 157 and Preston 1982: 215). This festival has become the most popular event of the year in the city of Cuttack. Thousands of rupees are spent at this time on expensive statues of the goddess, gifts for relatives, and elaborate parades through the streets of the city.

Durga has long been worshipped in this part of India, but never with such elaboration as in its current form. It appears that the present ceremonies have been imported from Calcutta in West Bengal, which is only a few hundred miles to the north. Reflected in this carnival quality of the Durga festival is a whole new dimension of mother worship which has emerged in Orissa since 1960. The earlier role of the goddess as an extension of the power and authority of the feudal kings seems to be giving way to a commercialized folk style of worship. The popularization of this once solemn festival is more than just the revitalization of an old tradition. Changes of a more profound nature are evident here. This new religious phenomenon poses some important questions about religious change. Here we see broader social changes phrased in a religious idiom. Why has mother worship become the vehicle for this kind of change? Is there something about female deities which easily accommodates to problems associated with urbanization? What is the nature of this emerging style of goddess worship?

Chandi Temple is an ideal place to study this pattern of change because it is the focal point for goddess worship in the city of Cuttack. Here is a relatively new temple which has managed to sever ties with its feudal past and has established an independent source of economic support. How is this economic independence related to the new style of goddess worship which is emerging in the city? Why has this kind of change happened here and not in other temples? By examining the social structure and sacred rites in Chandi Temple it will be possible to throw some light on the broader spectrum of religious change associated with the cult of the goddess.

THREE

PATTERNS OF PATRONAGE

THE RECENT VACUUM LEFT BY THE DECLINE OF ROYAL PATRONAGE
in Orissan religious institutions has produced an open arena
where the new mercantile classes, the educated elite, and government bureaucrats vie for authority. This struggle for control and
prestige is traced here through the history of patronage in
Chandi Temple. This small religious institution has become a
microcosm of larger forces presently emerging in urban Orissa.
The shift from a feudal patronage to a public trusteeship, along
with controversial issues related to the definition of a secular
state, is an intriguing commentary on the transitional status of
modernization in contemporary India.

Chandi in Her Urban Setting

Cuttack has all the characteristics of a major Indian city. It is
the largest center of commerce in Orissa with a population of
nearly 200,000 people. The city is located where the Mahanadi
River bifurcates before it empties into the Bay of Bengal thirty
miles away. This fertile coastal region is the major rice producing
area of Orissa. Cuttack is also located on the main route between
Calcutta and Madras. Because of its central position in trade
the city was the administrative headquarters for the government
of Orissa, until the new capital was built at Bhubaneswar thirty
miles to the south.

Bose has argued that towns in Orissa do not represent a "true
process of urbanization" because most of the people working in
them still draw on sources of income from rural landed estates.[1]
At the turn of the century O'Malley (1906: 40) described the
attachment of Orissans to rural life as follows, "The Oriya
appears to have an inherent aversion to town life; he will not
voluntarily leave his hereditary fields, and even when forced to
betake himself to a town, he strives to reproduce his village life
in his new surroundings." This is no longer an accurate picture.

Urbanization has rapidly increased since the breakdown of large rural landholdings. As a result of land shortage private properties have suffered from critical fragmentation, forcing many young people to turn to the city for income. Thus, a new urban orientation is gradually replacing the older attraction to rural life.

Cuttack is constructed like many old Indian cities. The main streets are linked in a series of chains connected in wide meandering circles, criss-crossed here and there by drainage canals and narrow side streets adjacent to remaining agricultural enclaves. The Westerner feels as if he is in a large collection of villages that grew together and were connected, more by accident than by design. Superimposed over this earlier impression are the straighter lines left by British colonial rule, such as the well-planned western side of the city which is occupied by colonial mansions that have been converted into government buildings or residence quarters for high officials in the civil service.

The older neighborhoods of the city are scattered along narrow roads. People here identify strongly with the local temples they support. Some of these neighborhood temples receive sizable subscriptions from rich and established patrons in the locality. Usually these temples have special festivals during the year when poor people and children are fed. Daily ceremonies are rarely held at fixed intervals, so that rituals may occur whenever a person of the neighborhood decides he wants to offer something to the deity. Neighborhood temples often have no landed property, except for the temple site itself, and are frequently administered by one or two families of priests, along with loose oversight by an ad hoc committee of influential people in the neighborhood.

Only thirty years ago Chandi of Cuttack was a small neighborhood temple made of clay located between Cuttack's older crowded sections and the large estates of the landed aristocracy. Today the temple has been modernized and enlarged. No longer can it be classified as a neighborhood temple, since it has grown to be the most popular place of worship in the city. This is partly due to the expansion of commercial establishments into the once quiet neighborhood where Chandi Temple is located. However, there are other reasons for the sudden growth of this small religious institution.

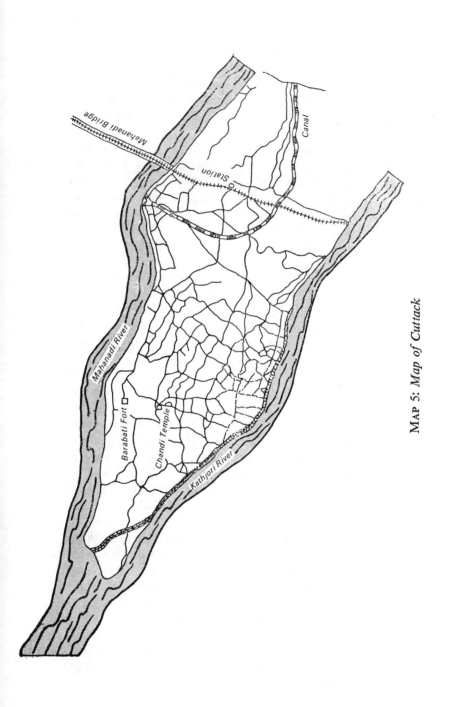

MAP 5: *Map of Cuttack*

Since it is neither an old established temple, nor a major pilgrimage site, what has been responsible for this rapid change? The best way to answer this question is to begin with a brief discussion of the traditional relationship of Orissan temples to their royal patrons.

Temples Without Kings

Religious and charitable institutions in the Indian subcontinent have been established, maintained and protected from early times by Hindu kings who regarded themselves to be specially charged with this divine duty. Before Independence the rajas of Orissa were the primary sources of patronage for Hindu temples. A serious vacuum emerged when these feudal princes lost their authority in 1947. No longer were the rajas the supreme guardians of the religious sphere. The result was a crisis in patronage forcing many temples to close and others to suffer serious poverty. Only a few continued to enjoy the support of the rajas. Others like Chandi of Cuttack were able to find new patrons to replace the old.

Before the rajas of Orissa were divested of their political powers their authority over a territory was justified by adopting a tutelary goddess (Mahapatra 1978). These female deities were associated with the founding of the raja's kingdom through legends portraying his successful conquest and right of sovereignty over local peoples, both tribal and peasant. Thus, the raja was identified with his kingdom through an elaborate set of rituals associated with his tutelary goddess. Many of these rajas took part in an annual ceremony which included army maneuvers meant to display the military prowess of the ruler in his partnership with the deity. At that time weapons were exhibited, along with the royal sword and other regalia. These were dedicated to the goddess. The raja would then go to the temple and make offerings. From there the royal family was followed to the parade grounds, which were usually located near the palace. The ceremony at the parade grounds culminated in target practice exercises. At the conclusion of this event the raja was expected to hit a target, then aim his arrows in all the directions of the compass to demonstrate his sovereign power over the territory. After this, drums were beaten and fireworks set off as a demonstration of strength to potential enemies who might violate his domain. The whole ceremony was a display of the raja's authority, reinforced through military maneuvers and sanctioned by the goddess, defender of the king and his people (Preston 1982: 214).

These rites have diminished since Independence, so that the goddesses of Orissa no longer act as defenders of the nobility. However, many vestigial rites of mother worship can be traced to this earlier integrating function of the goddess. Nor is there any evidence that mother worship is disappearing because of the decline of the rajas. Instead it continues to flourish, but with new patrons and in different forms.

The rajas had almost complete control over the internal affairs of the temples they supported. For centuries large tracts of land were granted to temples by these rich patrons. Since the patron's personal desires almost always went without question, his order was obeyed instantly. With the cooperation of the Brahmins the raja was able to secure almost complete control over temple income and property. Mukherjee (1953: 163) notes the supreme authority of the raja and the priesthood in relationship to the resumption of temple lands by donors. Verses like the following were sometimes added to votive records: "Whoever resumes the land given by himself or another is reborn in dung for 60,000 years. So it should not be robbed by wise men. Those who will obstruct the pious foundation will be guilty of slaying 10,000 tawny cows and Brahmins on the banks of the Ganga."

Thus, temples and patrons were once bound together through strong mutual obligations. The raja was Defender of the Faith and all major institutions depended on his endowments. This gave him the power to establish a division of labor in the temple, distributing specific duties to different castes.

Today the supreme authority of the raja has vanished. Village festivals that once brought people together under a single banner of fealty to celebrate territorial solidarity are still in existence, but the local rajas rarely participate directly in these festivities. At the town of Banki, for instance, thirty years ago the raja played an active role in the local festivals devoted to the goddess Charchicka. Today this raja does not visit the temple because it is too expensive to perform the elaborate rites expected of him. He no longer plays an important role in the ritual of the town. After his lands were reclaimed by the tenants who farmed them, the Raja of Banki was unable to wield any authority. As one raja expressed it, "There is a risk in trying to reclaim old traditions because of potential violence among local youths and other dissident groups." Another example of the decline of royal patronage was found at the town of Baramba where the young raja still sits on his throne, but retains little of the old ritual tradition that once linked his family to the temple of goddess Bhattarika. Until Independence there was a yearly procession where the golden deputy of this goddess was taken from the palace to the temple about three miles away. Palace and temple were linked in this old custom. Today there is no ceremony to tie the raja to the temple.

Decline of the Raja

Chandi Temple was established around 1880 on a small piece of land near the intersection of two major streets. The land was endowed by the family of the Raja of Rampur who played a central role in the temple's management until 1968. Today he is bitter about the new relationship of Orissan royalty to their former temples. He claims that religion in Orissa is becoming materialistic and people are exploited by priests who use their influence to prey on basic human weaknesses. A number of interviews with this raja revealed his feelings of frustration about changing patterns of patronage in Chandi Temple.

According to him, since Chandi Temple became popular it has become a crutch to reinforce human weaknesses. "It is no longer a question of Thy will be done. People have succumbed to the mystical powers of a few clever religious practitioners who have enslaved them." The family gods and goddesses of the ruling dynasty traditionally acted in the role of the guardian of the kingdom, defending the rajas in their struggles against the enemies of the empire. Today this function has disappeared. The Raja of Rampur believes this has happened because the royalty were "Brahmin ridden." "It was the human weakness of the rajas that brought the Brahmins into power. We rajas have always revolted against priests. They are not the proper medium for the propagation of religion." It was this dependency on the priests, the raja maintains, that further inclined the nobility to rely on the mercy of goddesses. "But we lost courage and the goddesses failed to answer our calls when the enemy took over." Thus, according to the raja, the royalty neglected their duties. "Under the Muslims thousands of temples were destroyed, yet the goddesses never helped the rajas to be victorious. All the rajas started off with their Chandis, and these Chandis let them down."

Even though the Raja of Rampur is losing control over Chandi Temple, he is still the patron of approximately five hundred other temples around his former kingdom. He comes to a temple's aid whenever one is in serious need. This is his traditional role. In 1972, for example, he claims to have given 20,000 rupees to these temples when their crops failed because of drought. The support of temples by rajas has played a major role in the cohesion of society. But this cohesive function, says the Raja of Rampur, is being gradually eroded as the Hindu Religious Endowment Commission (a branch of the state government of Orissa) becomes involved in local temple affairs. Until recently the Raja of Rampur was concerned about his temples. "I took great pride to see that the temples were given good care, but that pride is almost gone." Here he expresses defeat in the face of broad scale social changes that have undermined his previous role of sovereignty in the management of sacred institutions.

Contested Claims for Authority

A serious conflict over trusteeship has emerged at Chandi Temple in recent years. The triangular argument involves the family of Brahmin priests who claim the deity was installed in its present location by their forefathers. The Raja of Rampur contends that it was his grandmother who first endowed the temple land and had the icon of the goddess consecrated. A third claim is made by Chandi Temple's Board of Trustees which was set up by the Government of Orissa. They assert that it was the "public" who actually first installed the deity. Each party in this debate over rights to temple management has a legitimate argument based on one of several legends that have been advanced to explain the origin of the deity.

The priests of Chandi Temple claim that the image of the goddess was originally located about a half mile from the present temple site in Barabati Fort when the British conquered Orissa in 1803. According to this account, the British soldiers had difficulty conquering the fort because "Mother Chandi was protect-ing it." When the British learned that the goddess was helping the people of Orissa in their defence of the citadel, they tried to find out how she could be made powerless. Having heard that the goddess could be weakened by killing a bull and smearing some of its blood on their guns, the British proceeded to do so. As a result they captured the fort with little difficulty.

According to the priests it was not until 1878, some seventy-five years later that the statue of the goddess was removed from the fort to a place underneath a large spreading Banyan tree several yards from the present temple site. There a widowed woman worshipped the deity with great devotion. At that time the grandfather of the six Brahmin priests who presently serve at Chandi Temple moved the image of the deity to her present location and took over the priestly duty of daily worship. This priest then collected money from local patrons to build a small thatched temple. According to this version the raja was only one of several donors and not the founding patron.

The Raja of Rampur has a different account. According to him no one knows where the statue of the deity originated. The Moghuls probably destroyed whatever idols they found left in the fort when they conquered it. There were many of these images still laying around even after the British arrived. The icon of Chandi, according to the Raja of Rampur, was found near a large Banyan tree about a hundred years ago. A saintly man wanted to restore the deity, so the raja's grandmother built the original temple where the deity is presently installed. This was done around 1870. The raja's grandmother, who was a deeply religious woman, instructed her manager to appoint a local Brahmin boy who was good at singing and chanting (the grand-father of the six Brahmin priests) to perform the proper worship for the goddess. Five acres of land and a monthly salary of ten rupees were given to the priest for this service. There was a close patron/client relationship between the raja and the Brahmins, who were hired to worship the deity. The raja claims that there was never any question that his family was the rightful trustee of the temple until the Endowment Commission forced him out. It used to be that whenever the royal family went to the temple they were given special treatment. Everyone else was removed so the family could have the shrine completely to themselves. They

would send flowers and other offerings on every special ceremonial occasion. However, after the family of priests became
economically independent, they could do without the raja by
attracting rich merchants of Cuttack as patrons.

The President of the Board of Trustees has a third account
of the origin of the deity. According to him the statue of Chandi
is three to four hundred years old. This is documented in the
following history:

> People all over Orissa remember the role played by the deity
> in maintaining the independence of Orissa and the valour with
> which the attempt of the enemy [British] was frustrated in
> besieging the historical Barabati Fort. Since then the deity was
> removed to a small thatched hut in Sheikbazaar in the town.
> This place is now known as Cuttack Chandi Road (Executive
> Officer 1970:1).

The public official who wrote this account makes no mention
of either the Raja of Rampur or the family of Brahmins as
legitimate patrons. Instead, according to this source, the temple
was built largely by public donations rather than by a single
individual.

Here we see three contestants, each claiming his own legitimate
right to the control and management of Chandi Temple. The
origin legends are designed to serve the interests of the parties
involved. A paucity of historical evidence leaves the actual issue
of origin obscure, but that is not a concern here. The significant
point in all this is the use of origin legends as a means for
establishing legitimacy for wielding political power.

Toward a Centralized Patronage

The Endowment Commission of Orissa is trying to establish a
centralized patronage at Chandi Temple in order to clear up the
conflict between the raja and the priests. This government agency
has appointed a President of the Board of Trustees which makes
major decision about temple management. Also, the Endowment
Commission has assigned an Executive Officer to the institution
whose responsibility is to control all financial matters. The raja
it strongly opposed to this move on the part of the Government
of Orissa. He resents accusations of mismanagements of temple

funds and disagrees with the assertion that his family interfered in temple affairs. According to him, "Whenever the rajas built a temple the whole thing was designed with the priests as custodians. It was not the business of the raja's family to manage the temple." The raja continues to argue that the trouble began with the interference of the Government of Orissa.

The notion of a secular state which protects religious institutions from government interference is not originally an Asian concept (Smith 1963:22 and Miller and Wertz 1976:199). In India particularly, religion and political authority have always been inseparably entwined with each other. Religious reforms often parallel political changes. The lack of an ecclesiastical structure in Hinduism makes internal reform impossible to introduce formally into the system. For this reason the state has been pressed into service as the agency of religious reform. Its efforts at this, to some extent, have compromised the principle of separation of state and religion (*Ibid:* 29).

The decline of the feudal order has placed many temples in a precarious state of affairs. Therefore, government agencies have been given powers by legislatures to legally intervene and directly participate in temple management. This is not an entirely new idea. Under the British a number of large important temples were regulated and administered. The number of temples that have come under government control since Independence has greatly increased. Chandi of Cuttack is one among twelve thousand temples and monastic institutions in Orissa that presently are being governed under the Hindu Religious Endowment Act of 1951.[2]

Many of the temples in Orissa are in a constant state of litigation, with both priests and hereditary trustees under charges of misconduct and extortion. There have been official inquiries into reports of trustees treating temple property as their own and selling it at will. Charges have also been made of unorthodox bookkeeping, misappropriation of funds, and extortion of money from pilgrims (Aiyar 1960: 62-164). The following report on conditions at Orissa's largest shrine, the temple of Lord Jagannath, was filed by a government commission which was established to investigate corruption in Hindu religious institutions.

The affairs of Shri Jagannath temple are being managed very unsatisfactorily and the treasury is almost empty. Some cases are pending in the High Court and appeals are pending in the Supreme Court where the present Raja Sahib has applied for time having no money to pay even court fees. Temple valuables and properties are being sold away at a price much less than their market value. It is reported that a bungalow and the surrounding garden were transferred for Rs. 1,200... whereas its actual value is one lakh [Rs. 100,000]....The precious diamond necklace of Shri Jagannath has been taken away by the Raja Sahib. The gold ornaments reported to have been robbed from the temple of Shri Bimala Thakurani [consort of Lord Jagannath] have been found to be in the possession of a high personage. Recently a theft of Rs. 30,000 has been reported [*Ibid*: 386.]

Corruption of this kind has not escaped public scrutiny. Indeed, temples have become notorious places of scandal, fraud and deceit. In most cases the government has had little choice but to intervene. However, such intervention is not always called for, nor is it necessarily a panacea for the internal problems of temples. In a few cases the presence of the Endowment Commission has compounded the difficulties. Corruption in either direction is contagious. Government appointed administrators have occasionally been found participating in bribery, embezzlement and other infractions of the law. Trust boards are not, after all, beyond the natural pressures and temptations found in a growing bureaucracy.[3]

Under Hindu religious law the deity owns the offerings and endowments, not the priests or the people. The primary function of the Board of Trustees is thus to protect the deity's interests. The god or goddess is a perpetual minor when it comes to the secular field. It is for this reason that the deity must have a manager who will protect it from temple servants, hereditary trustees and other patrons who might claim to represent its interests.

An Executive Officer is usually appointed whenever a temple is taken over by the government. He is expected to mediate between the Board of Trustees, the Endowment Commissioner, and the priests. Though he is technically appointed by the

Endowment Commissioner, the Executive Officer is actually responsible to the President of the Board of Trustees, who delegates his duties. At Chandi Temple the Executive Officer has considerable responsibility. He must be present seven days per week to supervise the overall operation of the institution. Though his most important assignment is to prepare and control the budget, he is also expected to see that the rituals are performed on time, that there are sufficient materials available for the ceremony and that disorderly people are taken away. As custodian of the temple records, the Executive Officer records every offering in cash or kind and keeps all valuables under lock and key.

The Executive Officer at Chandi Temple is in an awkward position because of the contest between the three parties struggling for control over the institution. Thus, whenever he tries to implement a policy there is resistance from several directions. The occupant of this post in 1973 was a quiet person who constantly suffered from frustration in his role as mediator and temple manager. Almost every decision he made was blocked by either the trustees or the priests, weakening the government's attempt to centralize authority and control the institution.

Solidarity in the Priesthood

The priests of Chandi Temple are a single Brahmin family of six brothers. This is unusual, even for a small temple because of the convention that requires a second family of priests to celebrate the sacred rites in case of a death. Death pollutes all the members of a family and Brahmins are not supposed to worship the deity if a close kin has died. Yet, the fact that only one Brahmin family presides over the rituals at Chandi Temple tends to stabilize what would otherwise be a highly competitive struggle for rights to offerings among different families of priests. Most temples are constantly fraught with internal conflicts between different families of priests who compete for prestige and access to larger and larger shares of cash offerings.

Since the temple is less than one hundred years old the genealogy of the family of priests is quite simple. This contrasts sharply with other temples that have long histories. The priests of Chandi Temple live together as an extended family in a large dwelling about half a mile away from the temple. Approxima-

TABLE I

GENEALOGY OF THE FAMILY OF PRIESTS*

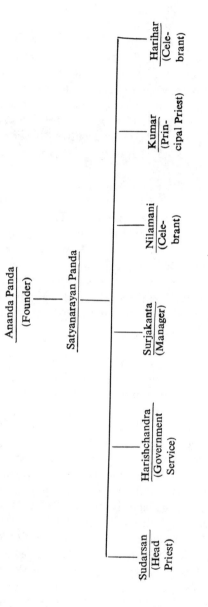

Ananda Panda
(Founder)

Satyanarayan Panda

Sudarsan
(Head
Priest)

Harishchandra
(Government
Service)

Surjakanta
(Manager)

Nilamani
(Cele-
brant)

Kumar
(Prin-
cipal Priest)

Harihar
(Cele-
brant)

*The names of priests have been altered in order to protect the identity of individuals.

tely forty-five people live in this household. When the father, Satyanarayan Panda, died in 1964 the six brothers inherited his full rights to ritual duties in the temple. The financial and moral support of the raja was no longer needed by the priests, once they had established economic self-sufficiency as the temple expanded in size and popularity. The father had already initiated litigation to claim ownership of the temple before he died. Therefore, the six sons inherited an uncertain future when the temple passed into their hands. And even though the struggle deepened when the Endowment Commission intervened, the family of Brahmin brothers stood undivided.

The priests consider the worship of the deity to be their paternal property and right. In the face of population pressures that have produced an overabundance of priests, this proprietary right to worship the deity has been parcelled out in most of the temples of Orissa, much as land has been, and its value has diminished accordingly. When there are numerous families of priests claiming traditional portions of the offerings, the solidarity of any single family is absolutely necessary. The six brothers at Chandi Temple have remained a joint household, thereby minimizing potential internal differences. This cooperation has given them a position of strength in combating the Board of Trustees and Endowment Commission who could otherwise diminish the margin of profit they reap and check their control over temple management.

Though Kumar Panda is considerably younger than his eldest brother, he has become the actual chief celebrant at the temple. This is because Kumar Panda is considered to be a mystic and generates a kind of charisma among devotees. Indeed, all of his five brothers refer questions about ritual matters to him. He is clearly recognized to be the principal priest and as such has the privilege of sitting on the Board of Trustees. He also performs all the most complex rituals on important ceremonial occasions and wields more influence than any of his brothers in the decision-making process. There is no conflict or jealousy evident about this difference in function between Kumar Panda and his eldest brother, who by tradition should be the leader of the family.

Of the remaining brothers, one, Harischandra Panda, is only marginally connected to the temple on special holidays when he takes charge of decorating the goddess with prescribed clothes and ornaments. Otherwise, he spends most of his time in the nearby city of Bhubaneswar as a government servant. Suryakanta Panda cannot perform the worship service because of a crooked finger that was broken in youth. It is traditional that Brahmins with physical deformities should abstain from performing sacred rites. This priest, therefore, abstains from performing rituals, but fulfills the function of supervising the temple servants. Nilamani Panda and Harihar Panda take turns with the principal priest in performing the daily rituals. Usually one priest celebrates for seven days while the others either take time off or help with the general management of the temple. All the brothers share equally in the profits received from offerings.

This collaboration among the priests gives an appearance of stability and calm which is absent among priests in other temples. People who attend Chandi Temple appreciate this cooperation because they are tired of petty conflicts seen among the priests in older traditional temples who compete for potential donors. The worshipper is left alone at Chandi Temple, receiving attention from the priests only if he seeks it. This lack of internal conflict in the priesthood is one factor that has attracted new patrons from the rich mercantile classes of Cuttack.

Conflict and Compromise

Though there is solidarity among the priests, conflicts still exist between the contending parties who seek to control Chandi Temple's economy. A written history of this dispute is found in the temple's official reports to the Endowment Commission. These records trace the struggle for authority back to 1939 when the first Endowment Commissioner tried to exercise jurisdiction over the temple. At that time, Satyanarayan Panda, father of the six priests, claimed that the temple was his private property. This angered the Raja of Rampur who filed a counter claim, and the whole matter went to the High Court. The raja and Commissioner made a compromise while the case was pending in the courts. The raja managed to get the Commissioner to recognize him as official Hereditary Trustee of the institution by conceding that the temple was essentially a public trust, rather than his own personal property.

After the Orissa Hindu Endowments Act of 1951 was passed

the priests filed a petition disputing the raja's new official appointment as "Hereditary Trustee." Another compromise was reached, this time between the Commissioner and the priests. This new compromise did not rescind the raja's official title of Hereditary Trustee. Instead, it added an additional title recognizing Satyanarayan Panda and his family as the rightful "Hereditary Priests" of Chandi Temple. This decision was unsatisfactory to both the raja and the priests. Appeals and cross appeals were filed against it by the two parties.

It was not until 1961 that administrative matters at the temple became critical. The priests and the raja were at loggerheads. Communication was breaking down. For this reason the Endowment Commissioner intervened to stabilize the situation. A new agreement was reached, providing for the appointment of a Managing Committee which would consist of the raja, a priest and five public members. A paid Executive Officer was then appointed to take charge of all valuables, collections of money and records. This new plan never actually worked because the Executive Officer was only a figurehead with little authority. He had almost no control over temple properties. As a result both the raja and priests continued to confiscate temple income and interfere in management. Allegedly the raja appointed temple servants at his will and deposited cash offerings in his personal bank account, while the priests continued to take saris, gold ornaments and other offerings which they believed to be their rightful payment for ceremonial duties.

Until 1968 there was great discontent and public clamor. Then a strong willed Executive Officer took charge. This man was a retired government servant who had worked in the Endowment Office. He knew exactly what to do in order to take control. There was no confusion in his mind about the public's right to the property of Chandi Temple. As he wrote in the temple records of 1969, "It cannot be believed for a moment that this historical temple was at any time the private property of any raja or Brahmin priest." The first step he took to gain control was to make a full inventory of all temple properties. This was done in the company of an Inspector from the Endowment Office. The priests were furious at first, but gradually accepted this active intervention in what they perceived to be their proprietary rights. The temple records were set in order, numerous improvements were made and the dispute between the raja and the priests was temporarily abated. However, this strong Executive Officer was only at the temple for two years. He was unfortunately followed by a series of less resourceful men who were unable to manage the temple with such ease and skill.

In 1968 the raja was finally eliminated from his bargaining position in temple politics when the Commissioner of Endowments issued an order declaring Chandi Temple to be public domain with non-hereditary trustees. A new Board of Trustees was appointed consisting of five members. This replaced the earlier seven-member Managing Committee and dropped the raja from his position of authority. Of course this move was contested in court.

Though the priests continue to be represented on the Board of Trustees by one vote, it is uncertain how long this will last. The old order is rapidly coming to an end. A new pattern of patronage is emerging in many Orissan temples. The principal players in the new order are those segments of Indian society, mostly rich merchants and the educated elite, who have inherited power and influence in the vacuum left by the fall of the feudal princes. Thus, the old tradition is being phrased in a modern idiom which opens the religious institutions of India to potential reformation, the full dimensions of which we have as yet to see.

Rise of the Mercantile Class

The mercantile class in Cuttack is made up of people from every caste. Those who patronize Chandi Temple, however, are mostly rich Marwaris, Bengalis and Gujaratis who have come to Orissa from other parts of India in the last hundred years. Marwaris are originally from the state of Rajasthan. Having established themselves in the booming economy of Cuttack, they have started to spend their excess profits on charitable institutions. These merchants traditionally worshipped the mother goddess in their home states. Many of them today will not begin their business day without having first worshipped at Chandi Temple.[4] It is the Marwaris who were responsible for purchasing a silver door for the inner sanctum of the temple, along with a new gate and a tile floor for the interior courtyard.

Many members of what could be classified as the "educated

elite" attend temple services. They include teachers, lawyers and government servants. Though some college students attend regularly, many have abandoned traditional temple worship, replacing it with a search for ultimate values in their educational studies. Others have joined new religious movements that have sprung up in Cuttack in the last several years. Though some of the educated elite contribute to Chandi Temple, this source of patronage is not as dependable as that of the merchants. Educated people tend instead to experiment with different styles of worship. Daily temple services are not usually essential to them. Though some worship at the temple every evening, most reserve their participation for holidays or special family rituals. This relaxed attitude about attendance appears to influence other family members who may be relatively uneducated.

A considerable percentage of Chandi Temple's income is derived from the middle classes of the city. Minor government officials, operators of small businesses and artisans contribute cash offerings, gold ornaments and other valuables to the temple's treasury. Since many members of the urban middle class in Orissa are originally from poor rural backgrounds, their new status is tenuous at best. Consequently they rely heavily on "good luck" in business ventures, educational opportunities for their children or upward mobility through the Indian civil service. The goddess is ever present in the minds of these still insecure members of the middle class. With her blessings it is possible for them to maintain a degree of insurance against the ever present possibility of financial ruin in case of a series of misfortunes. These new members of the middle classes usually have little land or savings to fall back on. For this reason any time they have a streak of "good luck" it is customary to thank the deity by giving something valuable to the temple. This source of income from the growing middle class, along with gifts from the rich merchants and educated elite, forms a viable alternative to the earlier pattern of patronage which typically remained in the hands of the raja and a few of his wealthy associates.

A new era has opened, loosening caste restrictions in some places and generating a new sense of religious freedom. According to one informant, "Religion is awakened in a modern new way. In the old days things were different. There was an emphasis on caste and our religion wasn't open to everybody, but now it is opening." The old structure is shifting. The new patrons are no longer an elite minority of landed aristocrats. They are now people of all castes and classes. Thus, patronage at Chandi Temple is spreading across broader socio-economic lines and integrating more individuals from a variety of different backgrounds. This process is gradual, yet steady and constant.

Changes in Temple Economics

A brief discussion of Chandi Temple's changing economy serves to clarify the new role of the mercantile class in the religious institutions of Cuttack. There were no reliable accounts of income or expenditures at Chandi Temple until 1968 when the Endowment Commission interceded. Up to that time only rough accounts were kept separately by the family of priests and the raja. Today there are yearly audits. Yet even these accounts are not entirely accurate because the priests keep some of the temple holdings in their private possession.

As late as 1950, when Chandi of Cuttack was still a small thatched temple the people offered articles of silver to the goddess. In recent years the deity is almost always offered gold ornaments. The shift from silver to gold accompanied an expanding cash income from individual donations and the sale of rights to temple concessions. Since government intervention in Chandi Temple, there has been a concerted effort by the Board of Trustees to increase its income, so that it is on par with Orissa's largest religious institutions which have vast land holdings.[5] Internal temple politics, however, have inhibited this plan. As far back as 1968 the Executive Officer suggested a solution by calling for more control of the priests.

> If a regular full-fledged scheme is framed and the high handedness and appropriation of income by the priests is fully checked, there is every possibility of increasing the income [from 100,000 rupees] to 150,000 rupees per year [Executive Officer].

In 1972 the temple had 350,000 rupees in the bank. The income for that year amounted to 180,000 rupees. This represents an 80 per cent increase from 1968 when the income was 100,000 rupees. By comparison to the large Orissan temples,

Chandi of Cuttack has an unusually large income for its size. The chief source of this wealth is from consignment fees paid for licenses of five concessions located within the temple compound. This amounts to approximately 60 per cent of the total income of the temple. Other large sources of income include fees for sacrificing male goats, cash gifts, and the sale of livestock offered to Chandi. Saris, ornaments and other offerings to the deity are auctioned to the public each year. The cash from this is deposited in the temple's treasury.

Most temples in Orissa have much larger expenditures than Chandi of Cuttack. This is because most of them have so many priests and other temple servants. Another problem in these large temples is the rising cost of maintaining temple structures. Consequently they are usually in debt because expenditures outweigh incomes. Unlike most rural temples, however, Chandi of Cuttack does not rely on income from the paddy grown on its land. This makes it immune to loss of income from crop failure or tenants who refuse to pay.[6]

Competition for Economic Control

The real point of contention presently at the temple is the issue of the dispersal of cash offerings made by devotees at the altar in a brass plate. Technically, according to temple regulations the deity is supposed to get 60 per cent of these cash offerings, leaving the priests with only 35 per cent. This formula is impossible to realize because the priests always have direct supervision over the collection plate. In 1972 the Executive Officer wanted to intervene in the collection. However, he cautiously avoided such a move for fear of trouble from the priests. Instead, the priests continued to take all cash offerings at the altar, leaving nothing for the treasury of the deity, despite government orders. In 1979 a new Executive Officer and his assistant have managed to curb most pilfering from the collection boxes. Nevertheless, he has been unable to control direct cash offerings solicited by the priests from devotees. Thousands of cases have been fought in Indian courts to check the power of priests who help themselves to temple properties and profits (Derrett 1966: 326). Since many priests have traditionally relied on a portion of temple offerings as their only source of income, it is understandable why they strongly resist any encroachment on what they perceive to be their hereditary rights.

Fifteen years ago the priests at Chandi Temple cooked whatever the people would bring as offerings to the goddess. It was an informal atmosphere, with no restrictions or special rules for the preparation of food, as long as it was cooked by a Brahmin priest. The temple kitchen is still maintained today, but there are numerous regulations about what can be brought to the temple to be cooked. In most cases the Brahmin cook is given money to purchase the ingredients for feasts. No one offers food to the goddess which has been brought directly from home any more. Only pastries and plantains from concessions located inside the temple can be offered to the goddess. This means that whoever owns these shops has a virtual monopoly on all purchases. There is no competition from outside. Since over 1,500 people attend the temple on an average day, purchases at these temple shops yield an excellent profit.

The quality of sweetmeats and other goods sold in the temple is maintained by vigorous competition among individuals who bid in an annual auction for consignment rights for concessions. Thus, a kind of market economy has entered directly into the temple sphere. This commercialism in the temple is carefully regulated by the Endowment Commission. The auction is theoretically open to anybody who has the money to pay fees for licenses to operate temple concessions. The actual profit reaped by the concessions is difficult to estimate because owners are not willing to make this information public. It is almost customary for store owners to claim they are operating at a loss. Even the roughest estimates, however, indicate that these small shops are very profitable.

It is difficult to know why the bids in the auction for these concessions went so high in 1973. An explanation was offered by the owner of the ghee lamp shop who tried desperately to hold on to his license at the auction,

I had a dream about Chandi. She woke me at night and said: "Bid in the auction as high as it goes. Do not fear. I am with you." The next day I thought this over. Since I am unable to count properly myself, I had someone else count my money for me. To my surprise I found that I had more than I thought

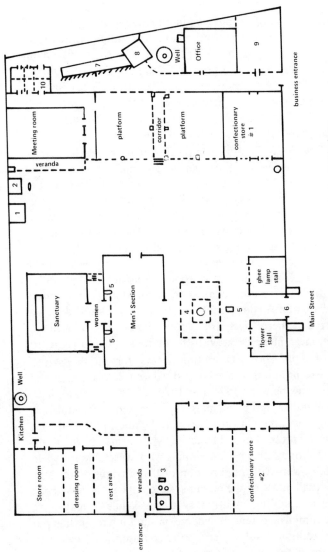

MAP 6: *Chandi of Cuttack*

1. Hanuman Shrine
2. Lakshmi/Narayan Shrine
3. Altar of the three Shivas
4. Place to offer ghee lamps
   and sacred fire pit
5. Donation boxes
6. Main entrance
7. Place to bathe feet
8. Hair cutting concession
9. Animals tethered
10. Six latrines

I had at first. One of my enemies wanted to drive me out, but the goddess wanted me to stay.

Private interests are often phrased in religious terms. The auction is no exception. The competition has increased significantly since 1971. It is no longer possible to keep a shop in the temple from year to year with only the support of powerful friends. Quality and ready cash are necessary prerequisites. The rules of the game are changing. A spirit of competition, even with one's own peers, and a knowledge of capital investment in the commercial economy are necessary for "success."

A brief revisit to Chandi Temple in 1979 revealed interesting new information on the auction system. Until 1975 the yearly auction was conducted before a large crowd within the temple premises. It was obvious that bidders had secret arrangements with each other. This public event became a power play among merchants seeking control of temple shops. A brief review of the data on concessions (Table II) reveals a drastic difference in prices for concessions between 1974 and 1975. Concession prices dropped considerably in 1975. This was due to a major change introduced by the Endowment Commission. The public auction was changed to a tender system where bids for concessions were placed in sealed envelopes. The person with the highest bid won rights to operate a temple shop. Operating rights for the two sweetmeat concessions and the ghee lamp store were sold at lower, but more steady rates between 1975 and 1979. The flower shop, haircutting stall, and sandal checking stall, increased considerably in value during this same period. This may be due to more honest competition for these shops. The tender system may have effectively blocked monopolies by individuals who were able to wield considerable power over the direction of the previous public auction. The overall effect of the tender system appears to have been to stabilize a spiraling inflationary trend. While it may have temporarily diminished temple income, in the long run it has put the temple economy in a very solid position. A review of the overall totals for income from concessions reveals a gradual increase to near the level once attained in 1972. Thus, it would appear that the new tender system has been an

TABLE II

RATES OF LICENSES FOR CONCESSIONS AT CHANDI TEMPLE

(in rupees)

Concession	1971	1972	1973	1974	1975	1976	1977	1978
Sweetmeats Store 1	18,000	28,000	40,500	46,025	25,000	25,500	25,550	26,000
Sweetmeats Store 2	—	7,000	19,050	23,950	15,000	15,050	15,125	15,150
Ghee Lamp and Incense Store	18,000	40,000	37,000	42,300	22,000	22,051	22,250	22,275
Flower Shop	—	12,000	10,000	10,000	7,000	11,050	14,250	12,000
Haircutting Stall	—	610	1,450	1,000	450	550	1,500	905
Sandal Checking Stall	—	300	300	500	400	500	1,805	5,200
Total Concession Income	36,000	87,910	108,300	123,775	69,850	74,701	80,480	81,530

effective leveling device; checking the control of shops by a few wealthy merchants and their associates, as well as removing the explosive open conflict potential in the previous public auction.

The development of a commercial base for Chandi Temple's economy does not imply the destruction of religious values. The vacuum left by the absence of the raja is more than adequately filled by the merchants of Cuttack. As new patrons, they reinterpret the symbol of the goddess by stressing new forms of worship. Though commercialism is spreading rapidly, there is no reason to believe that religion is declining. If anything the opposite may be the case. Religious festivities seem to be stimulated and sustained, as they always have been, by a strong undercurrent of economic activity.

Chandi Temple is thus growing into one of the important commercial centers of Cuttack. It has a savings account of 800,000 rupees, with an average annual income of approximately 100,000 rupees. Despite this large bank account, it is unable to expand in size. This is due to the scarcity of available land adjacent to the temple. Nevertheless, the present Board of Trustees continues to look for land nearby where they can build a *dharmasala*, charitable dispensary, Sanskrit library, and public reading room. Plans for these new facilities have been advanced for the last five years. The recent resolution of the court case over the dispute about patronage rights has made it possible to begin implementing these plans.

By 1979 the court case which had haunted the temple for forty years came to an end. It was finally decided that the temple was properly a public institution, but that the priests and the raja's family would both be represented equally on the Board of Trustees. This decision did not imply that either the priests or the raja were rightful hereditary patrons. Instead, it placed full responsibility for temple management within the hands of the pubic endowment. The raja, though not entirely without power, could no longer wield as much influence as he once did.

The decline of the raja has changed the structure of Chandi Temple and opened up new horizons for its future growth. How is this reflected at the symbolic level? The changes noted so far are flat and relatively meaningless unless we go to the very heart of the phenomenon of goddess worship itself. For these changing patterns of patronage are embedded in an elaborate system of symbolic rites which represent a sacred code of particular adaptive significance in Hinduism. Is there something about the rites and symbols of mother worship in India which can account for some of these changes? We have seen the close relationship between raja and goddess. We have also noted how the raja's function can diminish, while the deity remains an active agent of renewal.

Is this perhaps the key to unlocking this symbolic code? Is goddess worship essentially a means of celebrating the inevitable change built into the structure of the human condition? This crucial question can only be answered after entering into the sanctuary where the symbol of the divine mother is given homage each day.

FOUR

THE RITUAL PROCESS

A TEMPLE IS THE SUPREME LOCUS FOR *puja*, THE SACRED RITES of Hindu worship. As the home of the deity, the temple becomes a major focus for awakening the spiritual life in the community. This sacred structure is designed with extreme care. It must be clean, built according to prescribed scriptural formulae and constructed only at an auspicious time after consultation with an astrologer. Unless care is taken to observe these rules of purity it is believed the deity may be unsatisfied and will not be manifest with any degree of intensity at a particular site. A temple usually faces east and is laid out as a *mandala* (sacred diagram). Its most important part is the inner sanctum which holds the icon of the deity. This is called the *garbhagriha* or womb. Here is where the most sacred rites are performed. It is thus the heart of Hinduism.

Since the temple is a major place of devotion in Indian society, it is a perfect laboratory for the analysis of the rich symbolism which is elaborated in its ritual process. For here religious symbols become a model of reality in a way that makes the world comprehensible to people. Here symbolic codes are repeated, affirmed and disseminated to the community. These symbols create a special atmosphere where people of different castes and classes may come to find new strength and reorient their lives according to classical codes of conduct which have been passed from one generation to another for thousands of years.

Temple Atmosphere

The Hindu temple is more than just a simplified version of society (Dumont 1970: 28). It is also a place where everyday social reality can be temporarily transcended by the devotee. In fact the temple atmosphere is purposefully designed to allow for a great variety of religious expressions conducive to the worship of a deity. There can be no question that caste distinctions, pollution/purity norms and other features of Indian social organization are reflected in the temple, but also unique patterns are evident which temporarily suspend everyday social conventions. This is because the temple is both organically part of Indian social structure and separate from it—an intersection between two worlds, sacred and secular, which are never totally distinct from one another.

There are few rigid formalities at Chandi Temple. Though devotees must remove shoes and wash their feet before entering, they are free for the most part to move about the temple as they please. The temple is meant as a place for relaxation and enjoyment. According to one informant, "We are expected to feel some pleasure in worshipping at the temple." The idea of Hinduism propagated in the West emphasizes the ascetic austerities of yoga and self-control. But many Hindu temples do not fit this rigid stereotype. They are often noisy, boisterous and busy places with each devotee expressing himself in his own unique style of worship. The atmosphere at Chandi Temple is conducive to bringing the worshipper into the presence of the deity. Though there is always some measure of social convention maintained whenever people congregate, this is secondary to the more crucial experience of communication between man and deity.

Gestures of Worship

The most important rituals at Chandi Temple are held at night when hundreds of ghee lamps are placed by devotees before the image of the goddess in the main shrine. People typically visit several deities located in surrounding niches, offering personal prayers and asking for special favors. People talk freely in the temple. They purchase offerings, meet old friends and watch each other come and go. Men are usually found sitting on platforms night after night observing people, gossiping, exchanging ideas and absorbing the religious atmosphere.

All the senses are stimulated in the act of *darshan* (viewing the deity). There is a profusion of colors, sweet incense, garlands of tropical flowers, the smell of sweetmeats in preparation, and the odor of livestock that have been tethered in the courtyard. As the devotee approaches Chandi, he is given holy water and the sacramental leaf of a special plant (bel leaf). He is touched by the assistant priest who applies vermillion to his forehead. Then, in turn, worshipper touches the feet of the priest at the end of the ritual in order to get some of the *shakti* or sacred power that is believed to exude from the body of the Brahmin who has just completed the service. Drums, bells, conches, horns, and prayers fill the temple with variegated sounds. The whole human body is exercised as individuals genuflect, sing and prostrate themselves on the ground.

As the ritual builds in gradual cycles it contains and resolves the outflow of emotions from devotees. At the climax of the *puja* the drums begin and people rush forward, peering into the sanctuary to observe the sway of the priest as he chants prayers and performs *arati* by waving a tray of one hundred and eight ghee lamps before goddess Chandi. At this time the women make high throaty sounds. The drama reaches a crescendo as the drums peak in intensity. Sudden silence follows. The priest, transfixed, walks with the tray of ghee lamps around the temple and the people gather about to put their hands over the sacred flames.

According to the principal priest at Chandi Temple, man and nature are mixed in the ritual offering of earth, fire, air, water and the flowers and fruits of nature to the goddess. This point was collaborated by other priests who were interviewed. The individual worshipper is free to express his feelings of joy, sorrow or ecstacy through a wide variety of religious gestures. It is not uncommon, for example, to see an individual gazing at the goddess with mouth open, eyes fixed in a semi-trance and perspiration on his forehead. People prostrate themselves full length on the ground, kiss the stone at the feet of the deity, rub water from Chandi's bath on their foreheads and utter prayers of praise and glorification to the deity.

Vision and Puja

The ultimate goal of goddess worship is to reach emancipation through total identification with the deity. This is attained through yoga and the recitation of sacred texts associated with the Great Goddess.[1] It is a dangerous path requiring careful attention to intricate ritual details. One mistake may result in serious consequences, such as illness or death. Therefore, only the most highly skilled priests who have been trained by experts should attempt the elaborate rites which are believed to yield enormous spiritual power.

The special *mantras* (prayers) recited for each deity are mystical symbols capable of bringing the goddess into the human world. These *mantras* are combined with *yantras* (magical diagrams) which are drawn on the floor. The *puja* (worship) should be performed with the priest sitting in front of one of these *yantras* inviting the deity to come into his presence. Here is the intersection between the human world and the supernatural. In this way magical diagrams, prayers, and precise rituals of purification function to invoke the goddess and initiate a moment of transcendence.

To see these rites performed by a skilled priest is an unforgettable experience because of its great dramatic impact. The *puja* for mother worship is like a magnificent dance, every movement of which is performed with perfect control. The symbols of the deity are delicately manipulated by the priest whose task is to bring the supernatural into the presence of the congregation. Kumar Panda, the principal priest of Chandi Temple, was a consumate master at performing these rites. Extensive interviews with him and hours of observation have yielded the following interpretations of this important dimension of mother worship. By cross checking with other priests and the classical literature it has been possible to establish the legitimacy of his interpretation of these rites. Many of Kumar Panda's visions and religious experiences could only be communicated through the language of metaphor. This is because these experiences defy description in ordinary language. As Kumar Panda expressed it on many occasions, "One may taste sweets, but who can describe the *essence* of that which is sweet?"[2]

One of the first steps in the *puja* is for the priest to transform his body into a microcosm of the universe. This is accomplished by combining the five elements represented within it. Kumar Panda explained the correspondences between nature and the human body: *earth* is equated with that part of the body below the waist; *water* is symbolized by the stomach region; *fire* is represented by the heart; *wind* is equivalent to the throat, nose and lungs; *sky* corresponds to the brain. As these elements are mixed together in symbolic rites, the priest is filled with divine power or *shakti*, which is the goddess herself.

FIGURE 1: *The Sri yantra. A magical diagram drawn on the floor to bring the goddess into the presence of devotees during worship.*

Thus, the priest imitates the deity, until gradually he becomes at one with the icon as the ritual proceeds. By awakening the divine forces within himself the priest rises to the cosmic plane and becomes receptive to the supernatural world. Once this has been accomplished he puts the spirit of the deity which he experiences inwardly into the external image or statue, making it divine. The statue of the deity is recognized then to be only an inanimate object until it is given life by the priest. The ritual is nothing more than this process of bringing the presence of the goddess out of the recesses of the soul and into the temple icon itself. This objectification of the deity is accomplished through a series of purification rites which demand rigorous control of the body through yoga and prayer.

All sacred rites start with the chanting of *OM*. This mystical syllable represents the essence of the cosmos. By repeating it at the beginning of a *puja* the devotee moves into a state of readiness for contact with the supernatural. Now he is ready to enter into the deeper regions of meditation where ideally a vision of the goddess is attained. Interviews with priests reveal that not all of them have a profound religious experience while performing the *puja*. Kumar Panda describes his inner vision during meditation,

After performing meditation and the ritual for two or three hours, lightening flashes before my eyes. I am dressing the Mother. I am at that time the Mother myself. It is as though I were doing all of these things for my own mother....When I worship I forget myself. I become the goddess. She who is *Ma* (Mother) is me. There is no difference between *Ma* and me. Water and the coldness of water, fire and the burning capacity of fire, the sun and the rays of the sun; there is no difference between all these things, just as there is no difference between myself and the goddess.

There is a remarkable similarity of inner visions of the deity reported among devotees. The deity is frequently described as appearing at first in the form of a luminous blue light (Miller and Wertz 1976: 23, 30). This illumination is explained as a result of an inner heat which is generated in the devotee's body as he meditates—a manifestation of the deity taking shape in man. The key to attaining this state of grace is total control of the physical body through yoga. First there is the control of breathing to reduce the rate of respiration and heighten consciousness. This exercise has a mild euphoric effect. The priest sits in a prescribed yogic posture (*asana*) which relaxes the body, but keeps it receptive to the transformations which are to follow. New states of consciousness similar to those in sleep are penetrated by prolonged inhalation and exhalation. These breathing exercises are known as *pranayama* and are intended to increase inner heat. By slowing down his normal respiration the priest moves inward to the deep recesses of his spiritual life and is prepared for a profound encounter with the deity.

Once the goddess has been invoked the ritual gathers momentum. The purpose is to make the goddess feel like a welcome guest who is invited into the home of the devotee. She is offered a place to sit, welcomed and praised. Next she is bathed, garlanded, ornamented, dressed in new clothes, offered sandalwood and incense. Then she is given a sweet drink, fed a meal, offered spices and warmed with the light of a fire. The same respect that is shown to human guests in a Hindu household is offered to the deity. This ceremony may last for only half an hour, or, in its most elaborate form, which is performed only on auspicious occasions, it may take several hours to complete.

Since the goddess is a sacred guest the priest must constantly purify himself. This is done in several ways. At certain points in the ritual he rings a bell and claps his hands to scare away ghosts and evil spirits which are divisive forces, threatening the purity and wholeness attained in the *puja*. The most important agent of purification, however, is water which is poured from container to container throughout the ritual. Objects are dipped in water. It is sprinkled on the items used in the ceremony, then scattered in all the cardinal directions to purify the place of worship. The priest also uses water to sanctify his body, by sprinkling it around the mat where he sits. These rites form an integral part of the *puja* because they maintain purity for the deity or divine guest who is the object of worship.

During the Durga festival Kumar Panda performs this complex ritual with the same intensity for sixteen nights in a row. Muscular spasms are visible in his body as his trance deepens. A broad smile of deep reverence for the beloved Mother comes across his face in the advanced stages of his meditation. Tears often fill his eyes while he sings songs of praise and strews flowers at Chandi's feet. These flowers hold special significance for understanding the adoration of the goddess. As Kumar Panda expressed it,

> What is a flower? It is my soul. It is my prayer. All of my Self is offered in the flowers. If we go to meet a person, first we must give him a letter of introduction stating the purpose of the visit. Similarly the ideas in the mind are expressed to the goddess with the help of flowers. My mind, my body, my life, my soul—all these things are given through the flowers. It is a divine medium. They are *divine* flowers.

The point of all these rites is to abolish multiplicity and fragmentation, to reintegrate, and to make whole. Self-control in the priest becomes so complete that all external stimuli are closed out of consciousness. The priest is unaware of the hundreds of people who may be watching him. Since a temple is never a quiet place, it is not easy for the priest to attain this state of total detachment. But once he approaches perfect concentration, everything external disappears into a hazy background as the encounter with the deity becomes paramount. To the observer this strict physical discipline looks exhausting, but Kumar Panda is refreshed and exhilarated by it. "It is divine, a release," he says. "The rays coming from the inner light charge me with a devotional spirit and I am never tired."

The Unity of Man and God

The point of such rigorous concentration is to reach a state of total unity between man and deity. This is accomplished both internally through yoga and by treating the deity as though it were a person. Whatever man does in this life, the same is true for the deity. This is the key to Hinduism. It concretizes the more abstract aspects of the supernatural so that ordinary peasant people, who have little time for lengthy meditations, can relate directly to the gods and goddesses. For this reason the deities participate in the same sequence of rituals that would ideally govern the lives of royal personages. The goddess, for example, is bathed each morning after she is gently awakened from sleep. Her teeth are cleaned. She is invited to her morning

meal and given an afternoon nap. At night when the people
have left the temple she is put to bed with loving gestures of
appreciation and gratitude. Throughout the year the goddess is
given cool drinks on hot summer days, taken on processions to
visit the temples of other deities and dressed in special clothes
to celebrate festival occasions.

All these services for the goddess are part of a reciprocal relationship between man and deity. This reciprocity is reflected
in food offerings. First are the sacred food preparations offered
to the deity at meal times. These are cooked by priests and may
be consumed by temple servants and distributed to devotees as
sacraments. Second are the offerings of sweetmeats and plantains by devotees who purchase these items from temple concessions. Devotees give these offerings to an assistant priest who
places them before the goddess. They are then blessed by the
priest and returned to the person who offered them. It is
through this exchange of food between diety and devotee that a
special relationship of reciprocity is established. Thus, the devotee receives confidence and reassurance about his own suffering in return for his offerings to the goddess. This reciprocity
is possible because gods and men partake of the same reality at
different levels. There can be no problem of distance between
man and deity when there is such a close relationship. A
Brahmin women describes this intimacy in her personal relationship to the goddess,

> We act in front of the deity like this. Suppose we wash our
> feet in the morning, take a bath, go to the latrine and clean
> our teeth. At that time we direct the god or goddess to do the
> same: "Now you go have your bath. Now brush your teeth.
> Now go to the latrine." In your way [the Christian tradition]
> the god is far away. We believe that god is with us. God is
> everywhere. God is here.

The worship of female deities is part of a life affirming tradition which incorporates the sensual aspects of life as part of the
sacraments. Through a gradual process of self mastery the
devotee integrates the opposites within himself; not by denying
or repressing his sexuality, but by full receptivity to the divine
creation which dwells within. Thus, sexual union between man

and woman becomes the symbol of creation, transformation and oneness with the divinity. The unification of Siva and Shakti, god and goddess, symbolizes the transcending of opposites within the devotee's body. According to Eliade (1958: 271), this is "...the reintegration of the primordial androgyne, the conjunction in one's own being, of male and female—in a word, the reconquest of the completeness that precedes all creation." Kumar Panda phrased this integration of opposites with the metaphor of electricity. To him the divine light comes about through the fusion of positive and negative polarities during meditation. "Light cannot come at once. By working and working the negative and positive are connected."

Since sermons are not a part of Hinduism, how is the public affected by these complex rites performed in the sanctuary? This question is not easy to answer because of the many levels of participation in the ritual by devotees. While some higher castes are aware of the deepest symbolic meanings in the rites, others understand the ceremony to be nothing more than an act of devotion to the goddess. However, despite these differences in interpretation among devotees, there is a common bond established by the depth of emotional intensity in the priest. A truly devoted and charismatic priest is capable of being transformed by the depth of his devotion to the deity. This transformation of the priest generates a divine presence in the temple; attracting more and more worshippers, until the place becomes a major focus of special divinity. The people are connected to the main current of Hindu devotion through the degree of a priest's spiritual attainment. Thus, sermons and theological discourses are unnecessary in popular Hinduism, since the symbolic code is being perpetuated and renewed primarily through *puja*. Each person participates vicariously through the priest and by worshipping the deity in his own particular way at home or in the temple community. The *puja* conducted in the inner sanctuary is only the core of a much larger symbolic process which extends beyond the temple and into the streets of the city.

Expansion of the Ritual Process

There are broader links between Chandi Temple and Cuttack city than the competition for commercial rights within the temple. Temple ceremonies parallel rituals conducted in homes, neighborhoods, and at main intersections in the city. Chandi is the patroness of many businesses and, as presiding deity of Cuttack, she is associated with all the city's major festivals. For most of six months every year, from July through December, there are successive religious festivals almost every two weeks. These come in waves. No sooner has one cluster of celebrations ended than another begins. And each festival involves a specific sector of commerce. For example, while furniture and clothes may be purchased more at one festival, sweetmeats and handicrafts may be featured at another.

Chandi Temple is a major focus for many of these festivals. It attracts large numbers of people who seek the blessings of the goddess. Many special shops are set up on the street immediately outside the temple. Beggars congregate to prey on temple clientele and ritual processions stop in front of the temple to honor the deity. Thirty years ago there was only one shop in the street in front of the temple. Today there are nearly a hundred concessions, all clustered around the temple's entrance. These include numerous grocery stores, tea stalls and repair shops. The rapid growth of these small businesses started about fifteen years ago and is continually expanding. Shopkeepers here believe it is auspicious to be located next to the Goddess Chandi who will bring them good fortune. The visitors who come to Chandi Temple and the rickshaw pullers who wait outside are the most frequent patrons of these small concessions. The temple is, therefore, an economic advantage to the small businesses. Since there is little available land, the competition for space is keen. There are many people waiting for a vacant space to open a business.

Due to the sudden wealth of Chandi Temple the rituals have become longer and more intricate in recent years. Studies of other temples have shown a condensation of sacred rites, along with diminished priestly duties in daily worship. This attenuation of the role of priests has been noted in the sacred complex of Gaya (Vidyarthi 1961: 106) and at Lingaraj Temple in Bhubaneswar, Orissa (Mahapatra 1971: 74-79). Fifteen years ago the elaborate rituals during the Durga festival were only performed for nine days at Chandi Temple. Today the same rites have been extended to sixteen days. The temple is able to afford this ritual growth because of the larger staff, an increasing number of pilgrims and a bigger budget.

The Jagannath Temple at Puri plays an important role in Orissan religion because it provides a model for the ceremonies conducted in other temples. The auspicious and inauspicious dates for performing temple rites are often determined by the Jagannath Temple. Still, each temple has its own idiosyncratic customs which may vary from the Puri model. But in most cases these are only minor variations on the main theme which is designed by an elite group of priests and astrologers at Puri who represent the ultimate in ritual authority.

Compared to other shrines in Orissa, Chandi Temple relies very little on Puri as a center of ritual authority. Only the customary dresses used to decorate the statue of Chandi during the fall Durga festival are designed after those used in Puri. And though the temple generally follows prescribed dates for festivals suggested by the authorities at Puri, there is also considerable accommodation to the Marwari community in Cuttack who customarily celebrate festivals a few days before or after the Orissan pattern. In many instances Chandi Temple extends its ritual calendar to cover both Orissan and Marwari schedules. Also, since Chandi has no direct ritual association with Jagannath, there are numerous festivals celebrated at Puri that are omitted here.

Several of the rural festivals associated with goddesses and the agricultural cycle are absent from Chandi of Cuttack because of its urban setting. Nor does Goddess Chandi leave the temple in processions to visit other deities in nearby shrines. This lack of a procession, which is unusual for a goddess temple, does not seem to have a negative effect on attendance. People come to the goddess. She does not go to them And since restrictions on temple entry are almost non-existent, there is no need for Chandi to come into the streets so the lower castes can participate in ceremonies.

There are few Hindu festivals that are isolated from others. A single rite is usually part of a chain of festivals which are linked together so that the whole ritual year forms a unified pattern of religious celebrations. The ritual calendar is associated with seasonal changes. As rites and festivals combine and sometimes fuse there is a confluence of traditions that must be studied as interrelated aspects of one massive whole. Thus, a single ritual or cluster of rituals should be understood as part of a complex Hindu festival network. *Bali Jatra,* celebrated in December, is a good example of this multiplex linkage. Not only is it an auspicious time to worship the ancestors, it is also remembered as the time when Orissan men went off to trade their goods in Southeast Asia. At Cuttack an additional dimension is added because the festival has become an annual fair and also a time to remember the coming of the Bengali Saint Chaitanya to the city. Furthermore, the festival is linked to other festivals that come before and after it, forming part of a complex festival network synchronized through astrological time with different phases of the moon.

Durga Puja in Cuttack

Durga Puja is a major link between Chandi Temple and the city of Cuttack. This fall festival celebrates the destruction of evil by the goddess. Chandi is a form of the goddess Durga who is the presiding deity of war. Durga Puja is celebrated in most parts of India for nine days as part of *navaratri.* It is not clear why this festival lasts for sixteen days in Cuttack. Every town and village in Orissa celebrates Durga Puja. The festival at Cuttack is the biggest and most popular in Orissa. It is attended by approximately 150,000 people who come from all over the state. The festival builds to a crescendo in the last three days when there is much festivity, gift exchange, and finally a large procession of over one hundred life-size statues of various deities which have been skillfully carved out of clay. These costly and beautiful replicas of the deities are located throughout the neighborhoods of the city. Caste associations, neighborhood committees, merchants, and groups of students pool their money in order to pay the artisans who specialize in constructing these images.

On the final day of Durga Puja the statues are carried through the streets of Cuttack by lower castes. All the images are gathered at a prearranged time in a central bazaar where they are judged for their beauty and intricacy. This contest brings considerable prestige to the sponsoring group that wins. The procession then continues to the two rivers bordering Cuttack, where one by one the images are thrown into the water. The crowds cheer when they see the statues disappearing into the currents.

This is followed by city-wide dancing and singing in the streets. The custom of submerging the images of deities in water is found throughout India. Since Hindus believe that the invisible is reached through the visible, an image is only an instrument with no value once it has filled its purpose. The immersion ceremony signifies the impermanence of the material statues, and functions as a symbolic way of cooling the heat believed to be generated by the ritual (Babb 1975: 235). It also has the practical effect of keeping artisans who carve these images employed each year. If the statues were not thrown into the rivers the thriving business of making them would disappear.

The impact of Durga Puja on the economy of Cuttack is considerable. The bulk of the yearly income of many commorcial enterprises is made during the last three days of the festival. This is because people spend thousands of rupees in exchanging gifts; saris are given to young girls, sweetmeats and special curries are purchased at temples, and people buy special ornaments associated with this holiday in neighborhood shops.

Each evening during Durga Puja the goddess in Chandi Temple is dressed in one of her sixteen aspects. Thousands of visitors crowd into the small shrine to pay their respects. The ritual reaches a series of peaks on the final three nights of the festival. On the first night the deity is dressed as Saraswati, Goddess of Learning. Approximately four hundred goats are sacrificed the next night when Chandi appears as Kali. Finally, on the last night of the celebration the goddess is dressed as Durga, conqueror of Mahisasura, the Buffalo Demon.

The recent increase in popularity of this festival has been one factor in making Chandi Temple the major focus of religious activity in Cuttack. Since the decline of the rajas this commercial style of street ritual imported from Bengal has rapidly spread in Orissa's urban centers. Chandi of Cuttack provides an ideal nucleus for this modern style of Hindu worship, partly because the temple is emancipated from the control of its feudal patron. The new commercial patrons who are replacing the raja have helped to centralize and focus the religion of Cuttack on a single religious institution.

Most of the statues of the goddess which are paraded through the streets are brought to Chandi Temple as a gesture of respect for the presiding deity of Cuttack. Almost every Hindu in the city visits the temple at least once, and usually several times during the course of Durga Puja. But most important is the animal sacrifice which is held here. This is a dramatic highlight of the festival which attracts thousands of people to Chandi of Cuttack. No other temple in the city sacrifices animals on such a large scale.

The Ritual Sacrifice

Sacrifice is a major cornerstone of Hinduism. It is widely believed that a person's desires can be fulfilled by sacrificing an animal to a goddess. Sacrifice takes many forms; clarified butter, a product of the sacred cow, is poured into the sacrificial fire as a burnt offering. In ancient India horses were offered to the deities, but this practice was too expensive and eventually became extinct. There is also evidence of human sacrifice having been performed in some goddess temples.[3] However, today this practice has been abolished. Only animal sacrifice remains. These include buffaloes, goats and chickens. Animal sacrifice exists throughout India. However, it is particularly prevalent in Bengal, Orissa, and parts of Assam.

In the past the number of animals sacrificed in eastern India was staggering (Chakravarti 1972: 93). Recent resistance to blood sacrifice has reduced the numbers of animals slaughtered. Unsuccessful attempts have been made in parts of India to stop this custom through legislation. Gandhi was a persuasive voice against animal sacrifice. As a result of his influence, many temples either banned sacrifice or substituted pumpkins, cucumbers or gourds in place of animals. Some of the popularity of ritual sacrifice also has to do with the degree of Brahmin influence in an area. Kosambi (1962: 91) shows how animal sacrifice may be performed hesitantly when a temple has been identified with high caste Brahmins.

In the villages, there are obligatory blood sacrifices, unless the cult has been brahminised by identification with some puranic goddess, in which case the sacrificial animal may be shown to the goddess but has to be cut up at some distance. Rarely, a bloodless offering may be substituted.

Animal sacrifice has also diminished for economic reasons. Even the rajas of Orissa who once supported animal sacrifice cannot afford it on the grand scale they once did. Few people today are able to afford an animal as large as a buffalo to be sacrificed to the goddess.

In 1972 an unusually large number of animals were sacrificed at Chandi Temple during Durga Puja. Over five hundred goats and thirty chickens were offered to the goddess. People stood in line for hours outside the temple waiting for the ritual to begin. An estimated crowd of over ten thousand waited in the streets, on balconies and inside the temple for this high point in the Durga festival. The small staff of priests inside the temple had been working since early morning and would not be finished with their duties until dawn of the next day. The priests had been attending to the needs of devotees and performing rites for the goddess all day long. The temple was being prepared to handle the large crowds that would attend the midnight sacrifice. For this reason there were police everywhere and certain parts of the temple had been cordoned off to prevent a crush of spectators. People were admitted only one at a time to pay their respects to the goddess. Everyone was tense in anticipation of the dramatic event.

On the night of the sacrifice Chandi was dressed as Kali, the black goddess. Unlike the more benign forms of the deity, Kali is intentionally portrayed as a frightening hag with disheveled hair, pendulous breasts and a garland of skulls around her neck. According to legend, Kali emerged from the forehead of the Great Goddess who became black with anger as demons came to attack her. In this form the Great Goddess is the embodiment of the fury which can be raised in the divinity under emergency conditions. For this reason Kali is associated with death, cemetaries, funeral pyres and the darkness of night. Kali is a powerful goddess, capable of doing enormous damage to people who cross her. If angered and not appeased, she may bring disasters, illness or death to her people.

It is interesting to note that blood thirsty manifestations of the divine mother are associated with the "unmarried" status of the goddess. Babb (1975: 223) observes that "As Parvati, Lakshmi, Sita, or Savitri she becomes a benevolent goddess, a giver of wealth and progeny, and an examplar of passive devotion to her husband." These forms of the goddess are never offered sacrifices. In her unmarried form the goddess inspires tremendous fear in her people. They offer blood sacrifices to cool her potentially destructive temper.

People stretched and pushed that evening to get a glimpse of Chandi in her dress as Kali. Some chanted prayers. Others sat quietly in meditation. A few were sweating profusely, crying, singing and had worked themselves into a state of trance.[4] At one point the frenzy of the crowd reached such a high level of intensity that several men and boys were pushed into the women's section. Police had to be summoned to return the men to where they belonged. In the struggle that ensued, a door was torn from its hinges by the pressure of the tense crowd.

The atmosphere in the temple reached an even higher pitch of excitation as midnight approached. Gradually the chanting, drums and gongs advanced to a crescendo. Simultaneously outside of the temple the history and meaning of the ceremony was being broadcast over a loud speaker. The crowds were given instructions on how to manage the goats which were waiting in the streets for the sacrifice. Then the temple bell began to ring as a sign that the ritual was ready to commence.

Suddenly the drums stopped. Everyone anxiously waited for the main gate to open to admit the first goat. After the silence the drums played with new intensity to announce the beginning of the ceremony. The crowd strained to see the first goat as it was led to the small platform where the sacrifice would be conducted. This was located near the main gate inside the temple compound some distance in front of the inner sanctuary, but within view of the goddess.

The first sacrifice was preceded by a ritual performed by two Brahmin priests which took about twenty minutes. Since the sacrificial animal in Hinduism is seen as an embodiment of the cosmos, special purification rites must be performed to sanctify the animal. Thus, holy water was sprinkled on various parts of the animal's body while the priests chanted prayers to release the goddesses which are believed to reside in the animal's limbs. Then the priests worshipped the goat by offering it flowers, incense, food and water. This was followed by a secret prayer gently whispered into the ears of the animal to sever the bond of its life and thereby liberate its soul. Finally the sacrificial

FIGURE 2 : *The Mahakali yantra. A magical diagram representing the goddess in her form as Kali, destroyer of demons*

sword was worshipped to infuse it with the presence of the deities. The goat was then placed in position by a non-Brahmin specialist who would perform the sacrifice. The drums increased to their highest pitch and the actual sacrifice was made with one stroke. It is auspicious to kill the animal with a single, sharp stroke of the sword.

The crowd was silent as the animal's head was carried to the altar and placed on the ground before the goddess. Then the doors of the inner sanctuary were closed so Kumar Panda could complete the ritual offering of the animal to the goddess. Sacred scriptures were invoked recalling the purpose of sacrifice:

She herself is called Mahakali, Mahalakshmi and Mahasaras-wati. She is the Great Goddess of all the worlds, the dispenser of merit and sin. One who worships the destroyer of Mahisha [the Buffalo Demon] becomes the lord of the world. One should worship [her] by offering sacrifice steeped in blood, by flesh, by wine, by salutations, sipping of water, fragrant sandal . . .with an attitude of devotion in all these acts. In front of the Goddess, on the left side, one should worship the great Asura Mahisha [demon] whose head has been severed by the Goddess and who has attained union with her.

While the animal's head was offered on the altar its body was returned to its owner who would take it home to share with family and friends. People were crying as they passionately recited prayers in honor of the goddess. Soon the inner sanctuary was opened so the remaining sacrifices could be performed. Nearly five hundred goats waited outside, but from this point on the ritual for each of these animals only took a few minutes. This is because the ceremonies conducted for the first goat were meant to suffice for all those that followed.

Some people became irritable due to the late hour and the pressure of the crowd. Tempers flared in the mounting tension and a struggle broke out among devotees who were waiting to offer their goats. There was disagreement about who would be next and over the amount of the temple fee for sacrificing an animal. Considerable pushing and fighting ensued at the main gate, followed by arguments which broke out in different parts of the temple among people struggling for a better view of the event.

At one point Kumar Panda temporarily broke his meditation and looked out from behind the closed curtains of the inner sanctuary to see what was causing the disturbance. After a while the problem was solved and the tension subsided.

Near dawn the complex sacrificial rites came to an end. The next morning the goddess was given a complete bath for purification. Then a meal of meat curry prepared from the goat sacrifice on the previous night was offered to her. This is done on only a few special occasions during the year. Usually Chandi is a strict vegetarian deity who is not offered meat dishes. It was explained by some devotees that meat is given to the goddess only to satisfy her helpers, the Chamundis, who are demi-goddesses needing blood sacrifice to keep them from attacking people. These Chamundis help the goddess to protect her people from evil spirits.

An estimated 70,000 people attended Chandi Temple during the last five days of Durga Puja in 1972. This large number of devotees is increasing each year. The temple is thus a place where the Hindu population of Cuttack can congregate to experience a temporary sense of community. People of every neighborhood, caste and occupation come together as children of the goddess, seeking her favors and celebrating the conquest of good over evil. The sacrifice is the most highly attended ritual of all, despite the fact that most people express their dislike of it.

At one time there were practical consequences of the sacrifice. It used to be that the meat was divided and distributed among the poor. This custom of sharing wealth at the time of festivals played an important role in the social structure by providing ritual and economic links between members of different castes. Today, however, these social ties have been weakened. The bodies of the animals which have been sacrificed are kept by the individuals who offer them. The temple retains the animal's head from which a brain curry is prepared and sold to the public. Even strict high caste vegetarians have been known to purchase this curry because it is believed to have curative properties, since it was ritually offered to the goddess.

Most of the people who sacrifice animals at Chandi Temple are from lower castes.[5] They usually offer animals to the goddess in exchange for some kind of personal help. Among the most frequent reasons for sacrifice is to get new jobs, to enhance fertility, to acquire money, to send children to school and for relief from illness. Most of these people are poor and have little recourse to other means of solving problems. They rely on the intervention of the goddess to turn the course of events in their favor. Sometimes even people from higher castes offer animals to the goddess, but this is rare and may be masked from public attention because of the strong sanctions against sacrifice among intellectuals, students and bureaucrats. A few cases were reported of high caste people disguising their identities by sacrificing animals through hired servants.

Most people dislike animal sacrifice and express serious opposition to it. Though many of them participate in the ceremony, they say it is only out of curiosity. Why then does the practice continue to flourish in an urban center like Cuttack? In 1979 the Executive Office at Chandi Temple reported a marked increase in the number of animals sacrificed. According to this source over a thousand goats and several hundred chickens were sacrificed at the temple in 1978, representing a one hundred per cent increase since 1972. This increase is noteworthy because it implies that modernization does not necessarily result in the fading away of old traditions. In fact, sometimes customs like sacrifice become embellished and elaborated in urban settings. Perhaps newly urbanized people suffer from even more anxiety and frustration than their rural counterparts.

People who support sacrifice say it is an ancient custom which pleases the goddess and should be continued. Lower caste people often see the sacrifice as the exchange of an animal for a human life. They believe that the goddess likes blood. This substitution of animals to protect human beings is an interesting example of how sacrifice operates as a mediating device to cool the wrath of the goddess. Those who oppose animal sacrifice think it is sinful, antiquated and irreligious. As one man expressed it, "The goddess is mother of us all and she doesn't like blood sacrifice. Animals are also her children." This rational approach to sacrifice is probably a reflection of the effects of modern education, since many of the ancient Hindu scriptures clearly encourage it.

In the late 1940s sacrifice became a source of conflict at Chandi Temple. Some students and merchants tried to stop it by protesting in the streets. This caused considerable trouble and could have exploded into a riot, if it had not been for several priests who were able to explain its antiquity and scriptural legitimacy to the opposition. Since that time there have been other minor attempts to stop the sacrifice, but these have not been successful. This is because those who openly oppose sacrifice do not get enough active support from the public. Despite the fact that people dislike the custom, tampering with the sacred rites of Hindu temples is a dangerous and unpopular enterprise in India.

A ritual sacrifice is never meant as a violent act against a particular animal. The ceremonies that surround the event are intended instead to establish a symbolic relationship between man and god. The animal's life is offered to the deity as an act of love, thanksgiving or conciliation. It would be a mistake to equate everyday slaughter for food, with this higher dimension of the ritual sacrifice. Thus, the meaning of sacrifice may be missed by those who find it repulsive or brutal. It is neither "primitive" nor "barbaric," but rather an expression of special significance for devotees who strive to establish a sense of harmony with the cosmic order.

There are many dimensions to the sacrifice in India. Its symbolic content varies from one village to another and people are motivated to conduct it for a number of reasons. Yet, beneath all this diversity is a common thread of meaning which is reflected in both the sacred scriptures and at the folk level. It establishes hope where there is doubt and fear. The Hindu sacrifice is also concerned with the reality of death and evil. Its overriding theme is the promise that ignorance will lose its battle with truth. This is richly symbolized in the lengthy Durga festival where the goddess is portrayed as Queen of the Universe with ten hands holding various weapons to defeat the ever present enemy. There is no illusion here that evil will be suppressed forever. Quite to the contrary, the forces of darkness cannot be destroyed completely, for these are also part of reality.

At first glance, the sacrifice may seem to be an anomaly in a modernizing society. However, this is not the case if one looks beneath the surface to its deeper symbolic meaning. The elaborate rites in the sacrifice are intended to make the animal a symbolic vehicle for communication with the supernatural. It is considered to be something of tangible value which the devotee is able to offer as a gift to please the goddess and aid her as she struggles on his behalf. Evil is thus vanquished only when man is willing to play his part in the divine drama. The animal offered to the deity is ultimately a symbol which man places on the sacrificial altar to redeem his soul from its inevitable fall into the depths of darkness, ignorance and despair.

FIVE

RELIGIOUS EXPERIENCE

THOUGH MUCH HAS BEEN WRITTEN ABOUT THE RITUALS OF Hinduism, little is known about the religious experience of the people. Symbols are embedded in social institutions, but they also operate in the psyches of individuals. For some devotees the goddess is a constant source of personal enlightenment, appearing in dreams and always there when needed. Others relate to her only in serious crisis situations.

Interviews conducted in Cuttack among devotees of the goddess attempt to answer several questions about the phenomenon of mother worship.[1] What is responsible for the sudden increase in attendance at Chandi Temple? Why do people devote themselves to the goddess? How is she experienced internally? Is there a cultural pattern evident in reported miracles? What is the effect of social change on this form of Hinduism? All these questions ultimately lead to the relationship of symbolic change to the Orissan goddess cult in general.

Temple Attendance

Until 1957 Chandi Temple was a solitary place attended mostly by people from the neighborhood. In the early days devotees attended mostly on Thursdays. By 1965 Saturdays and Sundays also became important times for worship as people adapted to a more urban time table. Today there is heavy attendance in the morning just before office hours from 7:00 to 9:00 A.M. But the largest number of people worship at the temple at night when they have finished the bulk of the day's business. The temple has adjusted its time table to this urban rhythm.

Virtually all informants noted a large increase in the number of devotees worshipping at Chandi Temple over the years. It is impossible to accurately estimate the extent of this increase. Everyone interviewed agreed that it had changed from a small neighborhood shrine to the major center of religious activity in Cuttack within a period of only thirty years. Why has this happened to this temple and not another? Its location is no more strategic than many others which are situated in even more densely populated parts of the city.

TABLE III
ATTENDANCE AT CHANDI TEMPLE

Typical Wednesday Hours	Males	Females	Total
6:30— 8:30 A.M.	82	38	120
8:30—10:30 A.M.	187	120	297
10:30—12:30 A.M.	80	65	145
Break			
5:00—7:00 P.M.	233	145	378
7:00—9:00 P.M.	387	300	687
Total attendance	969	668	1,637
Typical Thursday			
5:30—7:30 P.M.	939	833	1,772
7:30—9:30 P.M.	483	459	942
Total attendance	1,422	1,292	2,714

These data were collected by counting the people who entered Chandi Temple on Wednesdays and Thursdays. Wednesday represents an average day of temple attendence. Thursday is always the most heavily attended at this temple.

There are several explanations for this rather sudden expansion of attendance at Chandi Temple. In the first place, many inhabitants of Cuttack have come from villages and need to adjust to city life. They suffer from stresses created by weakened ties with kin, the insecurity of urban occupations, and new life-styles outside the traditional boundaries of caste. The anxiety generated by these adjustments finds release through mother worship. In Cuttack the Goddess Chandi is considered a powerful deity capable of relieving many of these stresses.

Modern work schedules appear to have shortened the average length of time that an individual stays in the temple. Few people can afford to spend several hours a day in prayer. Nor is there time to withdraw for a number of days and nights of penance as is the custom in many village temples. People who were interviewed had other explanations for expanding temple attendance. As one informant put it, "We have become more religious minded in these days of worry. There are other deities, but Chandi is worshipped more than ever before." The principal priest at Chandi Temple explains the increase in attendance by refering to the efficacy of prayer, "The public has power by repeating the name of the goddess, *ma! ma! ma!* The people are attracted by the strength of these vibrations from worshippers in the temple."

Another reason for the increase in temple attendance is the withdrawal of the raja from his dominant position as patron. The merchants who are replacing him help to popularize the temple by spreading the fame of Goddess Chandi as a bestower of good fortune and success in business ventures. Even though the priests, the Board of Trustees and the Endowment Commission disagree about many things, they concur without reservation on one point at least; that is, to maximize the temple's margin of profit so that new buildings can be constructed to manage the rapid growth which has taken place in recent years.

The Divine Light

Hinduism is a religion of rich imagery. Gods and goddesses are depicted in the temples, along the streets and in people's homes. Yet, for some these external symbols of the deities are only aids to the deeper experience of the supernatural which takes place inside the devotee. It is here at the experiential level that sacred images take on their most important function as focusing devices for the awakening of that element of divinity which is in each person. Even the most unsophisticated worshipper may use some form of inner image in the first steps of meditation. According to one informant to enter into the spiritual world one must "...worship the mother by putting her lotus image inside your heart. Then concentrate until she becomes part of you."

At the folk level the stone image of the deity is frequently believed to be the goddess herself. But this is not always the case. There are also educated and uneducated people of all castes who perceive the icon as simply a symbol of the deity. In this view the statue is but a physical means of lending substance to a more abstract, all-pervasive deity. The icon then is only an external guide to help the devotee concentrate during meditation. Those who believe the goddess is in the stone image often think that she comes out of the temple at night to either help people in need or visit other deities in the neighborhood. This more concrete conception of the goddess is characteristic of people who do not see her when they close their eyes to meditate. The follow-ing description of the inner vision of the goddess reported by a devotee is typical of individuals who see the icon as only a sym-bol of the diety,

> When I pray, the goddess is visible in my mind's eye. Tears come to my eyes. She stands near to me, stretching her hand in a sign of blessing. Sometimes I see an inner light too. It seems at that time that my heart is lighted up or that there is a light just in front of me.

Not all people interviewed reported an internal dialogue with the deity when they meditate. Many just recite prayers they have memorized which give them a sense of release. The experience of feeling "refreshed and light" after worship was reported on a number of occasions, especially among highly educated infor-mants who claimed to worship only for concentration of mind, rather than for material gain. As in the case previously cited, concentration on the image of the deity sometimes leads the worshipper into a state of peace and harmony accompanied by an inner light. "This light cannot be described according to its color," said one woman. "I see it as the light from the inner portion of my heart." An experience of this light may be follo-wed by the appearance of the goddess in a kaleidoscopic series of different manifestations, such as Kali, Saraswati, Durga and Lakshmi. Some devotees seek a vision of the deity in order to be cured from a disease or handicap. In these cases the person may go to a temple for a prescribed number of days, eat only the sacramental food of the goddess, meditate and sleep on a bed of straw. If the person has a vision of the goddess during this retreat, it is interpreted as a sign that his illness will be cured.

Many people reported that the goddess appeared to them in a dream during a crisis situation. There is a curious pattern to the appearance of the divine mother in these dreams. She is frequently manifested as a young girl wearing a long white sari[2] or in her frightening form as Kali, dressed in black, with wild eyes. In most cases she appears in order to reassure the dreamer of her help and then suddenly vanishes. People describe these dreams in great detail, always noting their astonishment and deep spiritual transformation afterward. Dreams of this kind are often shared among family and friends, particularly when something dangerous or threatening occurs.

Occasionally devotees report visions of the goddess while awake. Again, as in dreams, she appears suddenly for a short period of time, says a few words, then disappears. It is interesting to note in this connection that these visions of the goddess often occur at twilight when the individual is alone in the privacy of his home, or while on a country road or in a wooded area. The goddess as Durga has long been associated with the forest, twilight and shadowy regions. In every case the devotee reports an initial reaction of fear and surprise. This is followed by a feeling of overwhelming love for the deity. The person is left stunned by the experience and gradually recovers to integrate it into his consciousness. In every instance the goddess has a purpose for appearing, which in most cases is to make a statement about the need for people to have faith during "these days of trouble." The interesting feature of this proclamation to mankind, is that it occurs in the context of an individual's personal problems. Thus, a vision of the goddess seems to have the dual function of both helping an individual solve a problem and rendering a message to the world at large.

Goddesses are notorious for possessing people. Sometimes shamans who specialize in curing, consciously seek possession by the deity. But rumors of unwilling young girls being possessed by a goddess are rampant. This typically occurs while the girl is walking along a dark road or in a place where she is unprotected by relatives and friends. In most cases this possession has a damaging effect on the girl, who my become ill or despondent as a result. Though I heard several second-hand accounts of this phenomenon, none of these could be confirmed. The popularity of such stories probably reflects more about the folklore associated with the power of goddesses to intervene in everyday life, than it says about the actual number of people who are possessed. Goddess possession seems to occur more frequently in villages than in large urban centers.

A Refuge from Stress

One of the oldest functions of the goddess is to protect and defend her people from evil. We have seen how as Chandi, Durga or Kali, she destroys demons. Also in an earlier chapter we have noted how goddesses protected local rajas against invaders. For this reason the goddess is often depicted with weapons of war in her numerous hands. In the *Devi Mahatmyam*, a sacred text glorifying the goddess, it is written,

> The infinite Lord, Brahma and Siva cannot adequately describe her unparalleled glory. May she, Chandika, be pleased to give thought to the protection of the entire world and to the destruction of the fear of evil. . .We bow down to thee, O Devi, protect the universe (Shankaranarayanan 1968: 79).

A typical story reported in rural areas describes how the goddess defends her temple from thieves who break in to steal the golden ornaments. The robber invariably is struck by blindness or totally disoriented somehow as he leaves the temple. He then stumbles, becomes confused and is finally caught by the people of the village. Interestingly, even though the thief is beaten by the people, he is then released. These legends serve notice to potential thieves who might be tempted to abscond with some of the precious ornaments of the deity.

The most important reason for worshipping the goddess is to fulfill personal needs. A survey of Hindu temples conducted by Bhardwaj (1973: 162) in North India reports that mother goddess shrines are favored by pilgrims with specific personal or material desires, motives and problems. Devotees interviewed in Orissa had similar reasons for worshipping the goddess. As one person expressed it, "I had a desire in my mind, so I turned to the goddess for help." The individual may even make a special vow to offer the goddess something of value if his "desire" is granted.

Though people who move to Cuttack from the villages do not totally abandon their traditional life-styles, they must still face new pressures resulting from less reliance on caste and kin. According to Srinivas, "Urban life sets up its own pressures, and a man's daily routine, his place of residence, the times of his meals are influenced more by his job than by caste and religion" (1966: 123). People typically adjust to these new urban requirements by dividing their lives into compartments and rearranging the role of tradition to complement the demands of the city.

Devotees at Chandi Temple reported worshipping the goddess to alleviate stress from competition, alienation and dislocations associated with life in Cuttack. This is seen at the end of the day in the temple when people call out to the divine mother with tears in their eyes as they unburden themselves. According to one informant, "This is our soul. When a man falls down he cries out *ma* (mother). We do not utter the name of father when in trouble. At that time we turn to the mother."

The word *ma* is habitually repeated to bring the presence of the mother into consciousness. The repetition of her name is a source of peace to many who turn to her in their personal turmoil. "When I face trouble or feel sorrow," said one man, "I call the goddess. Then I feel I am being helped." To some she is the gateway to the distant, more powerful father. "If we worship the mother, then we can get to the father." To devotees who primarily worship the divine mother, she is usually conceived to be more powerful than a male deity. The key to goddess worship is an attitude of complete surrender. Gods are to be respected, but goddesses are entrusted with human frailties.

Not all informants compare the goddess to their own mother. Usually she is thought to be superior to the corporeal mother, having functions reserved for deities alone. However, like an individual's own mother who is expected to meet one's needs, the goddess is bound to fulfill the desires of her devotees. This is her most important purpose. As a result many miracles are associated with female deities, particularly spectacular cures of dread diseases. Even though modern medicine has spread throughout coastal Orissa, people continue to rely on traditional religious cures. At one time there were little shrines devoted to Sitala, Goddess of Smallpox, situated all over rural Orissa, but these have diminished in importance as this disease has come under control.[3]

It is believed by some that a person can be cured by eating the deity's sacred meal or by sipping water from her bath. Sometimes the goddess cures an illness by appearing when the person is in a state of twilight sleep. The following is an example of this kind of cure,

I was suffering from severe cholic. It was about twenty years back. The Civil Surgeon of the hospital in Cuttack advised that I have an operation. My father would not allow this. About a month later the pain became unbearable. It was midnight. I got out of bed and laid down on the floor where it was cooler. Before I was completely asleep I saw the goddess who was in the room with me. There was a great white light that came from the middle of her forehead. She told me not to worry, that soon my pains would be gone. Then the light from her forehead focused on my stomach. Instantly the pain disappeared. I stood up. Then fell to my knees praising her. Before I knew what happened she suddenly vanished.

Usually cures do not result from such spectacular appearances of the deity. Instead, the devotee may simply rely on the curative powers associated with food, sacred ash or holy water from the temple. These sacraments may become agents for miracles. Rarely today, however, does an urban devotee rely on religious cures alone. In most cases people take a combination of traditional herbs and modern medicines. The goddess is usually approached when everything else fails, as a last resort.

Sometimes older people, particularly from lower castes, bargain with the deity. Usually they promise to give the goddess something in exchange for a desired result. This bargaining illustrates the reciprocity between man and deity which may involve an attitude of coercion, typical of popular religion throughout the world (Weber 1922: 25). The following account from a seventy year old untouchable illustrates this bargaining attitude toward deities, "I was suffering from water in the belly. I said to Goddess Chandi, 'If I am cured, I will exchange the head of an animal in place of my own.' This was twenty-two years back. Since I was cured, I offered a ram at Chandi Temple." This woman was exchanging the life of the animal for her own.

Almost all people believe the goddess has power to cast out evil spirits that cause illness or madness. These cases usually involve women. The goddess presents herself briefly before the evil spirit which immediately vanishes in terror. Here the deity acts as an antidote to demonic possession, which many people believe to be the prime cause for illness.

A number of young adults who were interviewed expressed doubt about reported "miraculous" cures. To these skeptical informants curing through supernatural means is only possible because the illnesses are of psychological etiology, rather than physical. But skepticism can go even further. For example, a college girl of Brahmin caste who was a science major had an experience to convince her that what she called "blind belief" may be destructive,

> Once in a village where I was visiting, there was a man suffering from smallpox. The local people thought that goddess Kali was in the man. So they tried to cure him with religious rituals. This was all in vain and the man died.

Not only does Chandi fulfill the traditional function of healer, she is also expected to answer many of the other needs of devotees. People do not hesitate to ask her for money, new jobs and good health. These are typical requests from hundreds of worshippers who daily flock to her shrine to have their personal desires granted. They ask for promotions, "good luck" in many matters or a chance to see distant relatives.

As the stresses of modern life and the need for more cash, material goods and opportunities for upward mobility increase, people turn more to goddesses who have protected them for centuries from hostile forces like disease, famine and flood. The modern religious tradition does not reflect a distinct break with the past in regard to the function of the goddess. Instead, there is a widening of her involvement in the problems of people. This is because she offers hope, where there is doubt and despair.

Changing Attitudes about Religion

People interviewed in Cuttack had two basic opinions about religious change. Some were concerned that Hindu ethics and religious institutions are declining. A worried man expressed this view when he said, "I believe there is a material change in Indian religion. We make too much of material things and not enough of moral values. We are heading for disaster." Others believed that exterior changes do not seriously affect the religious tradition. This view was held by Kumar Panda who thinks that modern technology will improve Hinduism. He does not feel that religion is threatened by change, because, as he put it, "spiritual truth is inside each person." The inner vision of the deity, according to this view, can be attained whether one denies or accepts the world.

Though educated youth tend to patronize temples less than other people, this does not necessarily mean they are irreligious. Indeed, interviews revealed that skeptics continue to worship in their homes or in some of the new cults which have emerged in Cuttack.[4] If anything, educated youth are merely seeking new forms of worship and often turn to the goddess to help them in their studies. These new forms of worship have interesting implications for the future of Hinduism. Since 1970 a large number of prayer groups associated with two religious sects have sprung up in different parts of Cuttack. The Sai Baba and Aurobindo movements have attracted considerable attention from different segments of the community. Typically devotees of the Sai Baba movement are young, small businessmen who are attracted by the miracles performed by this South Indian holy man. Aurobindo followers tend to be more intellectual. Devotees of this movement are usually educated and often come from the ranks of civil servants, teachers and wealthier classes. Neither movement prohibits a devotee from simultaneously attending traditional services at Hindu temples.

Modernization and Religious Beliefs

The scientific worldview has penetrated to even the most remote parts of India, though naturally the cities have been most affected. Interviews with devotees of the goddess cult in Cuttack revealed widespread consciousness about the relationship of modern science to ancient Hindu traditions. Even uneducated informants expressed concern about integrating these different worldviews. Most people find it relatively easy to rationalize the two, but it is a more serious problem for college educated youth in particular. This is probably because they are most exposed to concepts of modern science.

Science is not foreign to Hindu thought. Even yoga is a kind of science which aims at control over the body. However, the Hindu idea of science is based on different premises than that in the West. It is a science that finds validity in essences, rather than in the external form and structure of things. Thus, it is not satisfied with pure description of how nature operates. Hindu science is ultimately at the service of religious principles. Its prime purpose is to bring an experience of the "divine essence" to the individual. Validity is established by the experience itself, which can never be exactly replicated by another person. Once the devotee has mastered a degree of divine consciousness, it is believed that he is capable of performing extraordinary, miraculous feats that transport him beyond the ordinary limits of his body. All the rituals leading to this state of divine grace and the many social, economic and religious institutions that support it, may change endlessly, but not threaten the sublime yogic experience which remains unchanged at the core.

The transmission of this esoteric wisdom is lodged in the relationship of master to disciple. If yoga masters were replaced by books, the guiding personal touch, so necessary to the attainment of higher consciousness, would be destroyed and the tradition lost forever. This does not appear to be a real threat today. But what of the common person who participates for the most part in the traditional Hindu worldview? His religious values are attained through a network of rites and symbols propagated in the home, temple and community. Today this religious worldview intersects with scientific values generated through mass media in schools, films, and social programs supported by the secular state. How does the common person relate to these two systems of value?

Unfortunately it is often assumed that modernity and tradition conflict. This is simply not true. The two worldviews can be reconciled, but not without a certain degree of ambivalence. Indeed, some people, who publicly reject traditional Hinduism, continue to practice it in the privacy of their homes (Miller and Wertz 1976: 97). Even the most highly educated people I interviewed found a way to integrate modern and traditional values in their minds. The following statement from an Orissan physicist illustrates one person's solution to the problem of integration,

At this stage in my life I find most of the traditional stories and myths without any base; but the *essence* remains and I will continue to believe in the goddess. There is no inherent contradiction between a scientific attitude and religion. They can always be harmonized. The *essence* remains. There are many dogmas and rituals. Those things apart, the *essence* in fact is not in conflict with any of the points of view of science. They are not mutually exclusive.

This informant later told me how at one time the goddess helped him to overcome a serious illness while he was taking a qualifying exam. This experience convinced him of the spiritual power of the deity. As a physicist he conceives of the goddess as a manifestation of energy. There is no contradiction between science and religion, if they are interpreted as different approaches to the same reality.

Less educated people cited numerous examples of scientific discoveries which were anticipated in Hindu scriptures. One popular notion is that the first airplane was known in ancient times by Rama who flew across the ocean from Ceylon to India in a flower chariot. The marvels of modern technology are no surprise to people who believe that anything is possible religiously. After all, if man has invented these modern methods of manipulating the world, it is only because the deities have allowed him to do so. From this perspective science and religion converge to form a worldview largely unperturbed by incongruency. Each person resolves this problem in his own way at the level of personal religious experience. Religious reform movements play only a small part in the actual change of worldview which is ongoing within the heart of traditional Hinduism itself.

SIX

THE CHANGING COMPLEXION OF HINDUISM

THOUGH GOODESS WORSHIP IS VERY MUCH ALIVE IN INDIA, many of the temples which have supported it are in economic trouble. At one time only the rajas could afford to endow temples with large pieces of land. Today the government alone has such wealth. In the case of an urban temple like Chandi of Cuttack it is cash, not land that is most useful for maintaining the continuity of the tradition. Large landholdings are difficult to administer and are fraught with conflicts. Thus, land in many ways is more burdensome than advantageous. The emergence of new social conditions in India since Independence have serious consequences for the future of Hinduism. We have seen how secular and sacred worldviews have been resolved and integrated in the religious experiences of devotees. Here we return to goddess worship in its institutional setting to consider its possible future role in the modernization of Hinduism.

Future Priorities at Chandi Temple

In 1967 Chandi Temple came under the skillful management of its first strong-willed Executive Officer. At that time the institution was in poor economic condition. Despite large numbers of devotees most of the temple's income was not being spent on the temple itself. Most of it was being taken by the raja and the priests. The Executive Officer wanted to change these conditions. He was interested in developing an economically strong institution. After considerable struggle he made the following entry in his annual report, "The institution is now on the path of progress" (Executive Officer, 1968). This idea of applying the notion of "progress" to Chandi Temple was based on the model of Tirupati Temple in South India, where income from patrons has been used to considerable advantage by investment in a college, transportation for devotees, and new quarters for pilgrims.

Chandi Temple is in an unusual position. While it has managed to develop a viable urban economic base, with large profits and savings, it is unable to expand its small quarters. The resolution of the court case means that previous internal obstacles to expansion have been overcome. Nevertheless, external problems persist; all adjacent lands are in the hands of persons unwilling to sell. If the popularlity of this institution continues to increase at its present rate there will be serious overcrowding problems at the time of big festivals. Thus, a top priority is to find larger facilities; otherwise eventual crowding conditions may impair the present relaxed and pleasant atmosphere that plays such an important role in attracting devotees.

The Board of Trustees are keenly aware of these potential difficulties. Nevertheless, though the temple's profits accumulate and remain unspent the trustees continue to foster the accumulation of profits. There can be no growth for this urban religious institution without money, a prime commodity which brings prestige, power and influence. There are serious questions, however, about the ethics of capital gains in temples. For example, a government commission which investigated corruption in Hindu shrines praised the intelligent investment of profits at Tirupati Temple in South India, adding this interesting cautionary note.

Scrupulous care should be exercised to ensure that the ever expanding activities of the temple which undoubtedly enhance the temple's popularity and income should not leave any right or wrong impression in the mind of the devotees that the temple is being run with a commercial slant or with a view to profit (Aiyar 1960: 189).

The present study offers an alternative to the idea that commercialism is a necessary threat to the sacrality of religious institutions. The case of Chandi of Cuttack suggests that a modern urban temple must remain open to the economic resources that are available in the city. Is the commercialization of Hindu temples a real threat to the values of Indian religion and society? Or is commercialism just another transformation in the adaptation of temples to economic realities? The solution to the conflict over the management of Chandi Temple, with its successful adjustment to a new set of mercantile patrons and the public Board of Trustees, suggests that income from commerce is a viable method of survival for Hindu temples in modern India. But how can serious problems of corruption be avoided? This raises the issue of safe limits for government intervention in religious reform.

Government Intervention in Religious Institutions

We have noted elsewhere how the large Indian bureaucracy is committed to controlling the spread of corruption in religious institutions. This corruption which has increased in recent years, is due to conditions of extreme poverty among priests, dwindling incomes because of land fragmentation, and poor training of temple servants. Disputes over tenure of temple lands are endemic in Orissa, causing constant conflict and discontent, especially in large institutions that have many priests who claim hereditary rights over certain portions of temple income. When these problems become too serious, government officials must intervene to mediate in disputes.

Legislative reforms have been implemented by some states in India to cope with growing public discontent with the corruption that results from these problems. For example, the officers of Orissa's Hindu Endowment Commission have suggested that guaranteed incomes for priests might be one method to check corruption. This is problematic because many temples would be bankrupt if all the priests were to be paid adequate salaries. Also, how would it be possible to assess a *fair* amount of fixed income for temples, since they differ greatly in socio-economic conditions? And once a priest's income is guaranteed, what assurance is there that he would perform his religious duties? At present the amount of money a priest makes depends on free access to temple profits. At least this motivates him to attend to the needs of devotees.

Another problem to be resolved involves disputes over tenure of temple lands. Plans are presently being made to pay temples guaranteed annuities according to a specific formula. This would exempt all tenants from paying for the use of temple lands, while giving adequate support to those religious institutions that have been dependent on land based income. Annuities would be guaranteed to the temples by the government and the tenants would become the owners of lands formerly belonging to these temples. Of course taking away temple lands would be very distrubing to priests who would consider this to be irreligious.

The most difficult problem is that of selecting and training a well qualified priesthood. For the Endowment Commission to intervene in the actual religious affairs of temples would be extremely controversial. However, the Endowment Commissioner of Orissa (1972) is considering legislation which would give this state agency power to help select sons of the priests whom they judge to be most suitable for worshipping the deity. The remaining sons would then be encouraged to go into other vocations. If and when such legislation is ever passed, it would be a major reform of one cornerstone of Hinduism. Also this would have far-reaching consequences for the individual freedom of Hindu priests in Orissa.

Recently land reforms have seriously affected the agricultural base of temples that rely on sale of crops grown on their lands for economic survival. As one man expressed it, "Our gods and goddesses are starving." Because of the poverty of land based temples the Endowment Commission has encouraged them to develop capital support from sources other than land. Miller and Wertz (1976:201) are skeptical about cash donations replacing land endowed religious institutions. They suggest that land is more secure than cash. This may be true for rural temples and monasteries, but those located in urban centers must either seek new sources of income or perish.

Lasting reforms must first take root with the people to be effective. As we have seen in Chandi Temple, set regulations for the management of an institution may go completely unheeded. There must be public support for planned change or it will fail. There is no question that something has to be done about corruption. But too much intervention can be disastrous. Urban commercial temples like Chandi of Cuttack may represent a solution to the crisis in financial aid to temples. One would expect in the future a parallel development in village settings, with perhaps the emergence of rural commercial temples that would gradually break with their agricultural roots and participate more fully in the spreading commercial economy of rural Orissa. This will take many years, but it is not beyond possibility. In the meantime government support may be necessary for many temples to survive.

Government intervention is not popular among priests. They complain constantly about reduced income from donations due to regulations set up by new endowment laws. As a result some-priests are encouraging their sons to take up other professions. They also claim to have lost incentive to improve the temples or the quality of worship because the management has been taken out of their control. If this is true, Hinduism could suffer seriously from an apathetic priesthood. So far at Chandi Temple there is no evidence of indifference among the priests. But what would happen if they were unable to collect enough direct cash offerings from devotees to make their extra hard work worthwhile?

Even with the discontent expressed among priests throughout coastal Orissa, there is no evidence to suggest the development of even a rudimentary ecclesiastical organization among them. The old tradition of leaving the problems of management in the hands of patrons persists. Instead of the raja, it is now the Government of Orissa that is left with these responsibilities. This state control of Hindu temples is not entirely new, but rather a perpetuation of older patterns found in the medieval Hindu states and during the British rule of India (Smith 1963: 109).

State *intervention* in the affairs of religious institutions is one thing, but state *interference* is another. As Smith warned,

Corporate freedom of religion would certainly suffer if the state were legally connected with Hinduism, in which case one could expect the creation of a state Ecclesiastical Department with vast powers of control over Hindu temples and probably over Muslim, Christian and Sikh institutions as well (*Ibid.*: 160).

There is still no all-India legislation concerning religious institutions, though the need for such unified endowment laws has been acknowledged by the Government of India (Aiyar 1960: 172). At the same time the government recognizes the difficulty of adjudicating a uniform system of endowment legislation on an all-India basis. The complexity and diversity of local customs make this task nearly impossible. Therefore, today each state has taken its own course, superimposing an essentially Anglicized legalism over its ancient traditional institutions.

Urbanization and Change

Modern Hinduism is involved in a process of weaving secular themes from the scientific worldview into its fabric. The new thrust in religious reform includes less emphasis on caste distinctions, a broadening of social welfare activities on the part of temples and increased use of Western technology in worship services. It is perhaps this last feature which has had the most profound influence on modern Hinduism. Rapid modes of transportation, for example, have made it possible for people to travel to many temples which were inaccessible only a few years ago.

The introduction of new technology in Chandi Temple has attracted many devotees. People are proud that the temple they attend has neon lights, fans, bus service and loud speakers. These are prestigious additions to the institution. As a result the temple is more comfortable than it was before. But convenience and comfort are not as important to worshippers as the increased aesthetic value attained through the use of lighting and loud speakers to heighten the drama of rites conducted during major festivals. The worshippers at Chandi Temple are also affected by the demands of modernizing city life. Rituals must begin on time. The temple can no longer operate as it once did, according to the whims of the priests. The public trustees have regulated the temple schedule so that it meets the needs of office workers, merchants and businessmen.

Urbanism and the use of Western technology are only minor factors in the larger pattern of religious change taking place in India today. Though new technology may be employed from outside, the process of ongoing change also proceeds through the renewal of old myths and rites from within the traditional system itself. This is perhaps the more important feature of contemporary Hinduism; its capacity to reinterpret modern problems in terms of ancient symbols. The cult of the goddess is one of the most convenient and appropriate vehicles for change.

Materialism and Goddess Worship

Singer argues convincingly that modernization does not pose

a dilemma requiring a rejection of either modern or traditional culture. "The problem faced by traditional societies is how to continue their normal cultural metabolism, that is, how to continue converting the events of history into assimilable cultural traditions"(Singer 1972: 406). The case of Chandi Temple presented here illustrates this ongoing process of cultural metabolism at work in modern India. Today the goddess in Orissa symbolizes not only the continuity of an ancient tradition, but also the growing prosperity and expansion of India's commercial life. The goddess Chandi is thus an agent of change for the people of Cuttack; offering her worshippers both a stable link with the past and a medium for modernization. This temple is no longer a quiet place for the pious, but rather a vibrant hub of city life. It is a place for relieving tensions, where people who have been cut off from family ties or caste affiliations can meet in a community of kindred spirits.

There is nothing unusual about the capacity of Hinduism to use traditional symbols as vehicles for change. As Singer expressed it,

The traditionalism of Indian civilization is *not* opposed to innovation and change, to modernity, to the foreign and the strange. . .India's traditionalism is rather a built-in adaptive mechanism for making changes. Essentially, it is a series of processes for incorporating innovations into the culture and validating them (1972: 404).

The idea that Hinduism is a "life negating" religion that denies the pleasures of the "good life" to its people is inaccurate and misleading. Basham (1966: 37) correctly notes that ". . .the quest for spiritual riches was always affected by a quest for temporal riches, for power, for the pleasures of the senses." Though asceticism remains today an ideal in most people's minds, it is widely recognized that materialism and affluence are legitimate goals in life. There is no validity to the notion of the "spiritual east and material west." Both spiritual and material live side by side as part of the same system.

Mother worship has long supported this intimate relationship between the material and spiritual aspects of life. It may very well be that this is the most appropriate form of Hinduism to help people adapt to the advance of the scientific worldview in traditional India. As notions of caste and duty yield to the insecurities that accompany a less prescribed life-style goddess worship will probably increase rapidly. As we have seen in the case of Chandi Temple, it is the goddess who specializes in soothing the anxiety of people who are victims of social change. Secular themes are easy to integrate in the goddess cult because it has remained essentially a folk tradition, which has operated at the margins of classical Hinduism for thousands of years. Even though goddesses have attracted the highest castes at certain points in history, they have always been a refuge for the dispossessed and insecure elements of Indian society. Today everyone is undergoing some degree of change and uncertainty. In the light of this, it is not surprising that mother worship has risen to such a degree of prominance in urban Orissa.

Perspective

There are obvious limits to the study of a single religious institution. It is only because Chandi Temple is the most focal center of religion in Cuttack that it has been possible to generalize beyond the neighborhood to the city itself. We have seen how goddess Chandi fits into the citywide Durga festival. We have also noted the participation of different castes and classes in the temple's social organization. Through all of this it has been suggested that mother worship is a viable instrument of religious and social change in urban Orissa. Chandi Temple has also demonstrated the adaptive advantage of a smaller, relatively modern religious institution, capable of adjusting to the changing needs of an increasingly more complex and sophisticated public.

None of this religious change could occur, however, if it were true that religious institutions in India are declining because of the advance of modernism. To the contrary, though some temples are declining, others are being revitalized.[1] Change is an inevitable feature of modernity, and Hinduism has always changed. If this weren't the case, it would have disappeared long ago. Perhaps the unique challenge today is the integration of the scientific worldview into the framework of traditional Hinduism.

The cult of the goddess is a vibrant force in modern Hinduism.

It thrives alongside the worship of traditional male deities with equal strength. And this is to be expected at a time of rapid social change. We have seen how goddesses are perfect vehicles for helping people to solve their everyday problems. But psychological reasons alone are not sufficient to explain the growth of this cult. We have seen in the case of Chandi Temple how mother worship is linked to the new mercantile patrons of the city. This change in patronage has played an important role in the growth of the temple's popularity. Perhaps the most significant explanation, however, is the one advanced by most people when they are asked why the goddess has become so prominent recently. People almost always refer to the four *yugas* (ages) of Hinduism. According to this conception of time, we have come to the last great epoch, the *Kali Yuga* (Age of Goddess Kali). This is the time when human beings become increasingly more corrupt, until the world ends in complete destruction. It is inevitable that goddesses should be worshipped in these final stages of human existence. Only the Great Mother is capable of combating the enormous forces of evil unleashed upon the world during this last dark age. For the Hindu then, the goddess is a ray of hope in the inevitable corruption of the present world, and the cult which has arisen around her figure is an appropriate sign of the dawning of a new age.

SEVEN

SYMBOLS OF TRANSFORMATION

CHANDI TEMPLE STANDS AT THE CONFLUENCE OF IMPORTANT social, psychological, and symbolic changes occurring in Indian society. The goddess is a master symbol embedded in a matrix of related symbols, all linked together to form an elaborate tapestry of myths and rites spreading across South Asia. Personal needs, aspirations and weaknesses are acted out in the temple arena where human and divine intersect most completely. The goddess is only one of innumerable models for adaptation found in Indian culture.[1] Though there can be no doubt ancient Indian symbols perpetuate and reinforce strong traditional values, it is misleading to think of them as mere conservative links to the past. This may be true in some cases, but traditional symbols are also capable of acting as agents of change.[2]

No religion would survive beyond its founder unless it were capable of sustaining a balance between continuity and change. Since there is no such thing as an entirely static society, a religious system which survives must not only be flexible enough to shift with changing needs, but also capable of building on earlier values to lend a sense of identity, legitimacy and solidarity to its adherents. This delicate balance between the past and present demands a degree of timelessness, endurance and adaptability not easy to attain. Indeed, many religious systems do not succeed at this task and consequently fall by the wayside in the experimental process of symbol making which is forever taking place in human societies.

Since its inception anthropology has been concerned with religious change. Nineteenth-century anthropologists spent considerable time constructing elaborate theories to explain various types of religious systems. The Western notion of "progress" was a basic premise upon which evolutionary schemes were built by such eminent scholars as Tylor and Morgan. They saw religious change as part of the more general evolution of culture through inevitable predetermined stages.[3] Later theorists abandoned the evolutionary approach to religion, stressing instead its various unique functions in different cultural settings. These functionalists often conceived of religious systems as cultural devices to bring about social cohesion. In this view religious change was slow to come and almost always at the service of the larger functioning whole.

Contemporary anthropologists who investigate religion in complex cultures find simple functional models generated from studies of small-scale societies inadequate. Complex societies demand more subtle theoretical tools for the interpretation of religion. For this reason there is an emphasis today on the role of symbols in religious systems. One of the most crucial questions is how religious symbols operate in the process of change. This problem lies at the heart of many contemporary studies stressing the symbolic dimension of religious change.

The ethnography of Chandi Temple presented here is an attempt to understand how ancient traditional symbols operate in the broader process of change in contemporary India. The goddess was found to be a vibrant model of growth and transformation, despite strong secularizing forces. This disproves the thesis that Indian culture is rigid, resistant to change and bound by inflexible tradition. Change does not proceed by the creation of an endless series of *new* symbols, technologies or models for reality. It must also occur within a familiar idiom to assure a meaningful thread of continuity with the past. That which is old is not necessarily rigid and unchanging. Indeed, if tradition were essentially inflexible it would be unable to survive.

A society like India cannot afford to throw away its rich heritage in exchange for a few dubious advantages promised by modernism. For this reason effective change in the subcontinent is expressed through the traditional symbols which have operated for so many thousands of years as adaptive mechanisms to unite people of divergent languages, religious and ethnic groups. Beneath the many differences found among the people of India is a strong unifying mechanism in folk Hinduism which combines and integrates different symbols in an endless maze of interlocking myths and rites.

Early observers used the sacred Sanskrit texts as sources to interpret what they saw in Indian society. This resulted in rigid and idealized concepts of Hinduism and Indian culture which were perpetuated in the Western world. Consequently, the caste system was misunderstood, oversimplified, and given entirely too much emphasis. Gradually fieldwork conducted by anthropologists has revealed a different picture of Indian life. Social mobility and patterns of change have been reported even in the most tradition-bound villages, isolated from contact with the Western world. The picture of Hinduism and the Indian caste system which is emerging from these studies suggests a highly variegated system of social organization embedded in a rich symbolic framework which is dynamic and constantly in a state of flux.

Srinivas (1966: 6) has used the term *Sanskritization* to refer to the process by which people of low caste change their customs, ideology and way of life in the direction of a higher caste. This is accomplished by individuals or groups who emulate the behavior of higher castes. Untouchables or members of a low caste may begin to use Sanskrit texts in their worship services, hence the term *Sanskritization*. They also may become vegetarians, change their names and refuse to interdine with other castes considered to be beneath their new assumed status. *Sanskritization* is usually a mechanism for upward mobility within the caste system phrased in a religious idiom.

If it weren't for this built-in method of social change many tribal people would never have been absorbed into Indian society. The interpenetration of religion and social structure provides an ideal vehicle for the gradual transformation of non-Hindu elements in Indian civilization. As we have seen in the case of Orissa the cult of the goddess has been a focal point for the upward mobility of tribal people through incorporation into Hinduism. Kulke (1976: 9) observes that Brahmins in Orissa encouraged Hindus to settle down among tribal cultures to enlarge their clientele, encouraging upward social mobility of tribes into the lower ranks of the caste system through *Sanskritization*. We have noted earlier how tribal goddesses were frequently Hinduized, acting as a bridge between folk and elite. Thus, for centuries religion has been a major channel for changes occurring in the political and social arenas as Indian civilization transformed and assimilated foreign elements into its system.

The complexion of Indian society has changed considerably since Independence. A colonial system with strong feudal overtones has given way to a gradual democratization which is spreading throughout the country. This emergence of democratic institutions, combined with increasing urbanism, has resulted in new avenues for change outside the traditional caste system. This is not suggesting that caste is no longer a viable instrument for change. Indeed, in many places *Sanskritization* continues to operate as a vehicle of upward mobility. However, new occupations, Western education, and more reliance on cash income have opened up other major avenues of social change in India. But wealth, education or prestigious jobs are not enough to satisfy people who are involved in upward mobility. They also seek religious sanctions for their new found status. For this reason people turn to traditional symbols like the goddess to give them legitimacy among less fortunate contemporaries and to orient themselves within the larger context of Indian society. Thus, social and religious change are still entwined with each other, despite the effects of urbanism and new priorities resulting from the altered role of traditional caste loyalties.

It was surprising to find such little emphasis on caste at Chandi Temple. Caste was not stressed nearly as much as in the village shrines surveyed. Nor was there any clear process of *Sanskritization* at work in the temple. People were not emulating higher castes for upward mobility. Instead improved status was attained either through devotion to the goddess (dreams of the deity, miraculous cures, and spending long hours reciting holy scriptures) or by some kind of achieved notoriety in working for the welfare of the community. Caste was not a major factor in the formula for upward mobility at Chandi Temple. Thus, the concept of *Sanskritization*, while useful in some cases, is a limited explanatory device for the analysis of change.[4]

The Chandi Temple study is an example of a symbolic approach to religious and social change. By looking at a master symbol and exploring its manifestations in different domains, it has been possible to see the connections between fragments of a vastly complex behavioral system. Symbols are devices for communication. As such they link together various parts of a cultural network. Unlike small-scale societies which can be studied comprehensively, special analytic tools are required to cope with the built-in diversity of a civilization. A major world civilization is never just an accumulation of different ethnic groups bound together by a common technology. It is much more than this. Basic organizing principles are at work within any civilization. And these can be studied by an analysis of the master symbols which permeate the system.

What does the study of Chandi Temple suggest about the role of symbols in religious change? Symbols simultaneously unify and divide people. Consequently they are frequently fraught with ambivalence. We have seen how the goddess may take either the form of the peaceful integrating Saraswati or the dark mother Kali who divides good from evil. But more important than this capacity of symbols to have a multiplicity of meanings is their ability to help people transform themselves into different human beings. It is through sacred symbols that man reaches into what he perceives to be another dimension in order to be refreshed. This source of renewal is important, not just to the individual, but to any social system. For it is only through personal transformation that society is able to absorb, incubate and give birth to new ideas with which it may experiment that man may continue to adapt and evolve. This is the way a society maintains itself as a dynamic system. Since symbols must be shared to operate among people, certain prescribed behavioral patterns are always associated with their perpetuation. Thus, an established symbol like the goddess carries with it customs and attitudes built up over many years. If symbols such as these are periodically infused with new meaning they may act as major vehicles for cultural evolution.

When societies are suddenly faced with new, sometimes devastating experiences (as in some cases of culture contact) traditional symbols may collapse. But this is not always the case. They may also take on a new sense of meaning or even be completely reinterpreted. The most universal symbols in the world's religions have evolved because of their capacity to remain viable even under the strongest pressures for change. The collapse of a religious system is often due to a rigid elite that refuses to adapt to contemporary changes in the culture at large. When this occurs conditions are ripe for revolution or a major reform movement.

India has faced many profound social changes within the last five thousand years. Its system of religious symbols have also changed. This is testimony to the great flexibility of Hinduism.

There is no reason to believe the present influx of Western ideas and technology in India will result in the same kind of secularism as found in other parts of the world. Here we are dealing with a long tradition of folk religion interwoven into the very fabric of the social structure. Hinduism is not only enormously rich and malleable, but has certain built-in adaptive mechanism the Western world would do well to study and emulate. Unfortunately, we know very little about Hindu temples. Yet these are the most significant social institutions of Hinduism and house the key symbols which encode major integrating principles of Indian society.

The study of goddess worship raises some interesting questions about the role of the feminine in religious change. The new women's rights movement in America has made us conscious that female symbolism has been largely repressed in Christianity. Except for the worship of Mary within Catholicism, there is little emphasis on sacred female imagery. We have seen how feminine symbolism in the Indian goddess cult helps people to face the pressures of urban life-styles. It is curious that the women's liberation movement in the Western world has not managed to bring feminine symbolism into the Christian godhead. Also, one would expect a revitalization of the cult of Mary within Christianity. While there have been some efforts along these lines, for the immediate future feminine symbols in Christianity will likely remain secondary to more dominant male divine imagery. One explanation for the general lack of interest in rekindling feminine symbolism in the Western world is that changes that occur at the social level are not necessarily reflected in the religious sphere. In other words, symbol systems are not mere reflections or projections of social realities. Thus, the liberation of women's social roles is not necessarily followed by a re-definition of the supernatural world. The symbolic level has its own unique domain, no doubt connected to social and psychological factors, but not *determined* by them.

While certain Indian goddesses may be equal, if not superior to their male counterparts, this does not reflect an accurate picture of Indian social structure. Though motherhood is deeply respected in India, women are not equal to men in the social sphere. We must remember also that gods and goddesses are supernatural. As such they share human characteristics, but exist beyond the reach of human nature. If they were mere reflections of human life, there would be no sense in turning to them for insight and solace in the face of overwhelming tragedy. Sacred symbols participate simultaneously in two worlds, human and divine. Consequently they are capable of assisting humans to aspire to become something more; thus, inspiring transcendence of the limitations imposed by the conditions of life.

The qualities of the feminine found in the cult of the Indian goddess are universal. These include protection, nurturance, earthiness, and surrender. Goddesses make the world bearable, yet they retain an element of mystery that people can relate to with ease. Thus, the symbol of the goddess is a major integrating device in Hinduism; at once providing a sense of security in the changeless eternal mother and that sufficient degree of uncertainty and flexibility necessary for adjustment to the changing demands of everyday life. This unification of opposites is characteristic of enduring religious symbols the world over.

The goddess stands at the center of a complex mythology, rich with ancient metaphors for survival. As a master symbol the figure of the Divine Mother constitutes a "root paradigm" at the heart of Hinduism. According to Turner,

> Root paradigms are the cultural transliterations of genetic codes—they represent that in the human individual as a cultural entity which the DNA and RNA codes represent in him as a biological entity, the species life raised to the more complex symbolic organizational level of culture (1974: 67).

Though master symbols or "root paradigms" may not change significantly over time, their articulation with the social structure must certainly change if they are to have social and psychological utility for human beings. We have seen in the case of Chandi Temple how change and continuity operate in a single symbol. This is testimony to the great strength, endurance and flexibility of Hinduism which even today appears to be absorbing and dissolving the potential dangers of Westernization. If there is one principle common to Hinduism, it is this great resilience, a refusal to be vanquished, despite constant waves of threatening political and ideological systems from outside. It is almost paradoxical that the major integrating factor of Hinduism is its very tolerance for diversity through a constant process of incorporation. Other religions would be torn apart by so much variability. Hinduism thrives on it.

NOTES

Chapter 1

[1]Ashoka's last campaign was conducted against Kalinga, part of present-day Orissa, in the year 261 B.C.

[2]For arguments that Hinduism is slow to change see Ishwaran (1970:192), Gough (1970:156) and Epstein (1971: 462). Studies of declining religious institutions due to secularization include Mahapatra (1971:23), Eisenstadt (1970:31-33) and Vidyarthi (1960:214).

[3]It would be irresponsible to claim that religion always plays an active role in modernization. This is clearly not the case.

[4]One of the best studies of a Hindu temple was conducted by Vidyarthi (1961, 1979). Also, see Mahapatra (1971, Jindel (1976), Appadurai and Breckenridge (1976), Sinha and Saraswati (1978), and Fuller (1984).

[5]Ten months were spent investigating Chandi Temple (1972-1973) with weekly excursions for comparative purposes to goddess shrines in the surrounding region.

Chapter 2

[1]For a more extensive treatment of this survey see Preston (1983a).

Chapter 3

[1]Personal communication with N.K. Bose in 1972.

[2]The latest legislation was passed in 1969, but has not been implemented because of a controversy over a basic flaw in its design (Executive Officer:1970).

It is impossible to estimate exactly how many temples there are in Orissa today. The Office of Hindu Religious Endowments has a small staff due to limited funds and is not able to index or contact all temples that by definition should be under its jurisdiction. In the city of Cuttack alone there are nearly fifty religious institutions under the jurisdiction of the public trust.

[3]For a full government level investigation into the roots of corruption in religious institutions and proposed measures for reform see Aiyar (1960-62).

[4]Vidyarthi (1961: 92) has noted the patronage of rich Marwari and Bengali businessmen at the sacred pilgrimage center of Gaya as far back as the early nineteenth-century.

[5]In 1960 Tirupati Temple in Andhra Pradesh had an income of over ten million rupees, with a reserve fund of three million. Many large

temples of all-India importance have annual incomes that exceed 500,000 rupees per year (Aiyar 1960-62:160).

[6]Traditional temples in Orissa were like royal palaces, with large landholdings and tenant farmers (Miller and Wertz 1976:7).

Chapter 4

[1]The most important sacred literature associated with goddess worship is the *Markandeya Purana.*

[2]Otto (1923:7) noted this metaphorical nature of the sacred which admits of being discussed, but cannot be defined.

[3]Human sacrifice was performed even during the early part of the twentieth century (Rawson 1973: 48). The temple of the goddess Kamakhya in the border state of Assam was famous for human sacrifices. The victims were volunteers, admired for their desire to be sacrificed and given special honorary treatment. Human sacrifice seems to have been performed for the sake of agricultural fertility (Eliade 1958: 305, 306).

[4]Spirit possession and goddess worship are closely associated in India. For a good treatment of this phenomenon see Freeman (1974:55-63) and Babb (1975: 136).

[5]Bhardwaj (1973: 184) also notes the attraction of lower castes to goddess shrines where blood sacrifices were performed.

Chapter 5

[1]The data presented in this chapter are based on lengthy interviews conducted among thirty devotees in Cuttack. I have also relied on informal interviews at Chandi Temple and rural goddess shrines in the surrouding region. A deliberate attempt was made to gather information on religious experience among people from a broad range of castes, classes, ages and educational backgrounds. Though this represents a broad spectrum of the goddess cult in Cuttack, it is not intended to be an accurate representative sample.

[2]This pattern has been also reported by Miller and Wertz (1976: 22).

[3]Sitala continues to be worshipped extensively in West Bengal (Bang 1973).

[4]An excellent study of Hinduism and contemporary youth was conducted in India by Ashby (1974: 70) who asserts that "There is little evidence that modern education leads an appreciable group to a complete or meaningful break with their religion."

Chapter 6

[1]Miller and Wertz (1976:180) studied religious change in the monasteries of Orissa. They noted that ". . .there is no general trend toward secularization of religious institutions. The reverse process, sacralizing,

has occurred."

Chapter 7

[1] I am grateful to Professor Cora Du Bois for many helpful suggestions in preparing this chapter.

[2] There is a rich anthropological literature on religious revitalization movements and social change to support this point. See Wallace (1966), Peacock (1968) and Worsley (1957).

[3] In recent years there has been a new interest in developing evolutionary schemes to understand religious systems. Unlike nineteenth-century theorists, the neo-evolutionary approach does not assume that all religions must evolve through a set of predetermined stages. Instead, the emphasis is on the correlation of particular religions with increasing levels of complexity in social organization. This kind of correlation does not imply the superior development of one religion over another (Bellah 1965).

[4] Another term frequently employed by social scientists to study change is *modernization*. This term is used much too loosely in the literature. Does *modernization* mean the introduction of Western forms of government, science, education and technology to a culture? Or does it refer to something which is new or contemporary? A clear distinction needs to be made here between what is meant by *modern* and *contemporary* because they may be quite different phenomena.

RECOMMENDED READINGS

TOPICAL WORKS

The best source for Indian mother worship is Agehananda Bharati's *The Tantric Tradition*, published by Doubleday and Company (Garden City, 1965). Also, Sir John Woodroofe has provided an excellent analysis of the rites associated with the cult of the goddess in his book *Shakti and Shakta*, published by Ganesh and Company (Madras: 1929).

Hinduism has been studied by many anthropologists. One of the best collections of articles on religion in India is Edward B. Harper's edited volume *Religion in South Asia*, published by the University of Washington Press (Seattle: 1964). An in-depth study of popular religion in India is Lawrence Babb's outstanding volume *The Divine Hierarchy*, published by Columbia University Press (New York: 1975). This book is an excellent introduction to contemporary Hinduism in central India. Recently one of India's largest shrines has been studied by C.J. Fuller, *Servants of the Goddess* (Cambridge: 1984).

Milton Singer's *When a Great Tradition Modernizes*, published by Praeger (New York: 1972), has become a classic work on religious and social change in urban India. Another classic is *Social Change in Modern India* by M.N. Srinivas, published by the University of California Press (Berkeley: 1966). In this volume Srinivas explicates his interesting concept of Sanskritization, a mechanism for upward social mobility in the caste system.

REGIONAL WORKS

A comprehensive treatment of contemporary religion in Orissa is *Hindu Monastic Life* by David M. Miller and Dorothy C. Wertz, published by McGill-Queen's University Press (Montreal: 1976). This volume is based on a study of the monasteries of Bhubaneswar, an ancient center of Hinduism and the new capital of Orissa. James Freeman has conducted research on village religion. Preliminary reports on his work are found in "Trial by Fire," *Natural History* (January 1974) and "Religious Change in a Hindu Pilgrimage Center," *Review of Religious Research* (Winter, 1975). Two recent studies by Freeman offer deep insights into patterns of religious change in Orissa. These are *Scarcity and Opportunity in an Indian Village*, published by Cummings (Menlo Park: 1977) and *Untouchable*, published by Stanford University Press (Stanford: 1979).

For a Full treatment of the Jagannath Cult of Puri see K. C. Mishra's *The Cult of Jagannath*, published by K. L. Mukhopadyay (Calcutta:

1971) and *The Cult of Jagannath and the Regional Tradition of Orissa,* edited by A. Eschmann, H. Kulke and G. Tripathi, published by Manohar Press (New Delhi: 1978).

BIBLIOGRAPHY

Aiyar, C.P. Ramaswami. 1960-1962. *Report of the Hindu Religious Endowments Commission.* New Delhi: Government of India.

Appadurai, Arjun and Carol Appadurai Breckenridge. 1976. The South Indian Temple: Authority, Honor and Redistribution. *Contributions to Indian Sociology,* 10, 2: 187-211.

Ashby, Philip H. 1974. *Modern Trends in Hinduism.* New York: Columbia University Press.

Babb, Lawrence. 1975. *The Divine Hierarchy.* New York: Columbia University Press.

Bang, B. G. 1973. Current Concepts of the Smallpox Goddess Sitala in Parts of West Bengal. *Man in India,* 53, 79-104.

Basham, A. L. 1966. *Aspects of Ancient Indian Culture.* New York: Asia Publishing House.

Bellah, Robert. 1965. Religious Evolution. In *Reader in Comparative Religion,* eds. William Lessa and Evon Vogt. New York: Harper and Row.

Bharati, Agehananda. 1965. *The Tantric Tradition.* Garden City, New York, Doubleday and Company.

Bhardwaj. Surinder Mohan. 1973. *Hindu Places of Pilgrimage.* Berkeley University of California Press.

Campbell, Ena. 1982. The Virgin of Guadalupe and the Female Self-Image. In *Mother Worship: Theme and Variations,* ed. James J. Preston. Chapel Hill: University of North Carolina Press.

Chakravarti, Chintaharan. 1972. *Tantras: Studies in Their Religion and Literature.* Calcutta: Punthi Pustak.

Chattopadyaya, Sudhakar. 1970. *Evolution of Hindu Sects.* New Delhi: Oriental Press.

Clothey, Fred. Pilgrimage Centers in the Tamil Cultus of Murukan. *Journal of the American Academy of Religion,* 40, 72-95.

Danielou, Alain. 1964. *Hindu Polytheism.* London: Routledge and Kegan Paul.

Derrett, J. Duncan M. 1966. The Reform of Hindu Religious Endowments. In *South Asian Politics and Religion,* ed. Donald E. Smith. Princeton: Princeton University Press.

Diamond, Norma. 1970. Fieldwork in a Complex Society. In *Being an Anthropologist,* ed. George Spindler. New York: Holt, Rinehart and Winston.

Dumont, Louis. 1970. *Religion, Politics and History in India.* The Hague: Mouton Publishers.

Eisenstadt, S. N. 1970. Prologue. In *Change and Continuity in India's Villages,* ed. K. Ishwaran. New York: Columbia University Press.

El Guindi, Fadwa. 1977. *Religion in Culture.* Dubuque, Iowa: William C. Brown Co.

Eliade, Mircea. 1958. *Yoga: I mmortality and Freedom.* Princeton: Princeton University Press.

Epstein, Scarlet. 1970. *Economic Development and Social Change,* ed. George Dalton. Garden City: The Natural History Press.

Eschmann, Anncharlott *et al.,* eds. 1978. *The Cult of Jagannath and the Regional Tradition of Orissa.* New Delhi: Manohar Publications.

Executive Officer. 1968-1970. Administrative Report of Shri Cuttack Chandi Temple. Unpublished Papers.

Freeman, James. 1974. Trial by Fire. *Natural History,* 55-63, 83.

————1975. Religious Change in a Hindu Pilgrimage Center. *Review of Religious Research,* 16, 124-133.

————1977. *Scarcity and Opportunity in an Indian Village.* Menlo Park, California: Cummings.

————1979. *Untouchable.* Stanford: Stanford University Press.

Freilich, Morris. 1970a. Fieldwork: An Introduction. In *Marginal Natives,* ed. Morris Freilich. New York: Harper and Row.

————1970b. Toward a Formalization of Fieldwork. In *Marginal Natives,* ed. Morris Freilich. New York: Harper and Row.

Fuller, C.J. 1984. *Servants of the Goddess: The Priests of a South Indian Temple.* Cambridge: Cambridge University Press.

Gough, Kathleen. 1970. Palakkara: Social and Religious Change in Central Kerala. In *Change and Continuity in India's Villages,* ed. K. Ishwaran. New York: Columbia University Press.

Ishwaran, K. 1970. Mallur: Internal Dynamics of Change in a Mysore Village. In *Change and Continuity in India's Villages,* ed. K. Ishwaran. New York: Columbia University Press.

Jha, Makhan. 1971. *The Sacred Complex in Janakpur.* Allahabad: United Publishers.

Jindel, Rajendra. 1976. *Culture of a Sacred Town.* Bombay: Popular Prakashan.

Kosambi, D.D. 1962. *Myth and Reality.* Bombay: Popular Prakashan.

Kulke, Hermann. 1976. Kshatriyaization and Social Change. Reprint of the South Asia Institute of Heidelberg University.

Mahapatra, L.K. 1978. Gods, Kings, and the Caste System in India. In *Community, Self, and Identity,* eds. Bhabagrahi Misra and James J. Preston. World Anthropology Series. The Hague: Mouton Publishers.

Mahapatra, Manmohan. 1971. Lingaraj Temple: Its Structure and Change. Unpublished Ph.D. dissertation, Utkal University.

Manual for Bhagavan Sri Sathya Sai Seva Organization. 1971. Madras: Fifth All India Conference.

Miller, David M. and Dorothy Wertz. 1976. *Hindu Monastic Life.* Montreal: McGill-Queen's University Press.

Mookerjee, Ajitcoomar. 1971. *Tantra Asana.* Basel: Ravi Kumar.

Mukherjee, P. 1953. *The Gajapati Kings of Orissa.* Calcutta: The General Trading Company.

O'Malley, L. S. S. 1906. *Bengal District Gazeteers: Cuttack.* Calcutta: The Bengal Secretariat Book Depot.

Otto, Rudolph. 1923. *The Idea of the Holy.* London: Oxford University Press.

Peacock, James. 1968. *Rites of Modernization.* Chicago: University of Chicago Press.

Preston, James J. 1978. The Commercial Economy of an Urban Temple in India. In *Community, Self, and Identity,* eds. Bhabagrahi Misra and James J. Preston. The Hague: Mouton Publishers.

———. 1980a. Sacred Centers and Symbolic Networks in South Asia. *Mankind Quarterly,* 20, 3: 259-293.

———. 1980b. Two Urbanizing Orissan Temples (written with James Freeman). In *Transformation of a Sacred City: Bhabaneswar, India,* ed. Susan Seymour. Boulder: Westview Press.

———. 1982. The Goddess Chandi as an Agent of Change. In *Mother Worship: Theme and Variations,* ed. James J. Preston. Chapel Hill: North Carolina.

———. 1983a. Goddess Temples in Orissa: An Anthropological Survey. In *Religion in Modern India,* ed. Giri Raj Gupta. New Delhi: Vikas Publishers.

———. 1983b. The Hindu Sacred Image: Its Creation and Destruction. *Anima,* 10, 1: 34-50.

Rawson, Philip. 1973. *The Art of Tantra.* Greenwich, Conn.: New York Graphic Society.

Redfield, Robert. 1956. *Peasant Society and Culture.* Chicago: The University of Chicago Press.

Sarma, Mohan. 1971. *Kamakhya.* New Delhi: Census of India.

Shankaranarayanan. 1968. *Devi Mahatmyam.* Madras: Ganesh and Co.

Singer, Milton. 1972. *When a Great Tradition Modernizes.* New York: Praeger Publishers.

Sinha, Surajit and B. Saraswati. 1978. *Ascetics of Kashi.* Varanasi: N.K. Bose Memorial Foundation.

Sircar, Dines Chandra. The Sakta Pithas. *Journal of the Royal Asiatic Society of Bengal,* 14, 1-80.

Smith, Donald E. 1963. *India as a Secular State.* Princeton: Princeton University Press.

Srinivas, M.N. 1966. *Social Change in Modern India.* Berkeley: University of California Press.

Trotter, Robert J. 1976. God: She's Alive and Well. *Science News,* 109, 7: 106-110.

Turner, Victor. 1974. *Dramas, Fields, and Metaphors.* Ithaca: Cornell University Press.

Vidyarthi, L. P. 1960. Thinking about a Secular City. *The Eastern Anthropologist,* 13:203-215.

———1961. *The Sacred Complex in Hindu Gaya.* New York: Asia Publishing House.

———1979. *The Sacred Complex of Kashi.* New Delhi: Concept Publishing Co.

Wadley, Susan. 1975. *Shakti.* Chicago: Department of Anthropology, The University of Chicago.

Wallace, Anthony F. C. 1966. *Religion: An Anthropological View.* New York: Random House.

Weber, Max. 1922. *The Sociology of Religion.* Boston: Beacon Press.

Wolf, Eric. 1958. The Virgin of Guadalupe: A Mexican National Symbol. In *Reader in Comparative Religion,* eds. William Lessa and Evon Vogt. New York: Harper and Row.

Worsley, Peter. 1957. *The Trumpet Shall Sound.* London: MacGibbon & Kee.

INDEX

108 *Index*